David Dorward

was born and educated in Dundee. He is a graduate in Arts and Law of the University of St Andrews, having carried out his legal studies at Queen's College, Dundee (as it then was) and having been apprenticed to a firm of solicitors in the city. After National Service at NATO HQ Fontainebleau, he practised for short time as a solicitor before joining the administrative staff of his old University where he remained for thirty-two years, eventuallly attaining the position of Secretary.

He and his wife (a retired solicitor) live in retirement in a village near St Andrews. He enjoys gardening, golf and music-making; he also travels extensively with his wife at home and abroad, often on visits to their two sons and two grandsons. He is glad of the leisure to pursue his lifelong interest in the meanings of names—personal and of place. *Scottish Surnames* and *Scotland's Place-names* are two others of his publications.

David Dorward

DUNDEE

NAMES, PEOPLE AND PLACES

MERCAT PRESS

First published in 1998 by Mercat Press
James Thin, 53 South Bridge, Edinburgh EH1 1YS

ISBN 1873644 795

Typeset in Times New Roman 11 point at Mercat Press
Printed and bound by Bell & Bain Ltd, Glasgow

Contents

Dedication   vii
Crawford's 1793 map of Dundee   viii-ix
Introduction   1
Names, People and Places   7
Envoi   151

William H Smith
Jan. 19TH 2018

Dedication

For Joy, my true and honourable wife,
also a Dundonian and proud of it

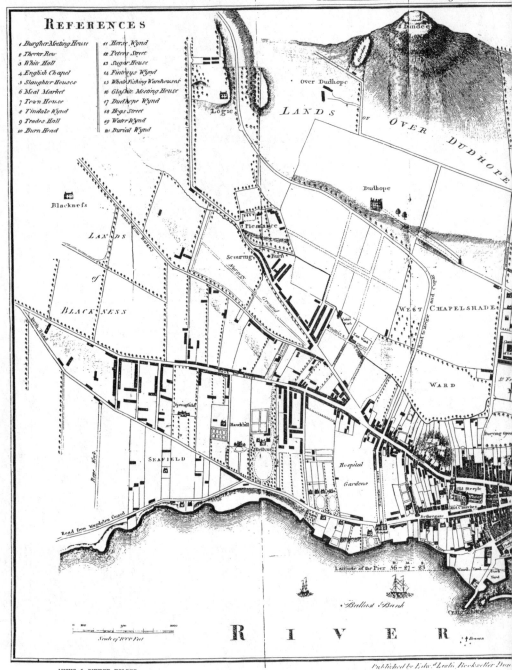

REFERENCES

1 Burgher Meeting House	11 Horse Wynd
2 Theater Row	12 Peters Street
3 White Hall	13 Sugar House
4 English Chapel	14 Fintrays Wynd
5 Slaughter Houses	15 Whale Fishing Warehouses
6 Meal Market	16 Glassite Meeting House
7 Town House	17 Dudhope Wynd
8 Tindale Wynd	18 Hogs Street
9 Trades Hall	19 Water Wynd
10 Burn Head	20 Burial Wynd

ANGUS & DUNDEE FOLDER

Published by Edw.ᵈ Leslie Bookseller Dun

William Crawford's map showing Dundee in 1793
(*National Library of Scotland*)

PLAN
of the
Town, Harbour & Suburbs of
Dundee,
With the ADJACENT Country.

From a Survey in February 1793 By
Wm Crawford & Son, Land surveyors
at Cameron Bank near Edinburgh.

Introduction

The history of Dundee, ranging in time from the prehistoric shell-middens of the Stannergate to the new Technology Park on the western boundary of the city, has been recorded many times over the years. But for the average person, chronological history is not an easy read, unless some end is in view or some particular reference is sought. Furthermore, academic history very often fails to give the flavour of the place, and many readers will find anecdotal lore as important as historic fact. There have been several comprehensive histories of Dundee, from the first historical account written anonymously in 1776 to the recent *Life and Times of Dundee*; even more has been written about the city's industry and commerce, and much (perhaps too much) about McGonagall. Pictorial records of the old city are copious; books such as Lamb's *Old Dundee* have preserved in magnificent line-drawings the features of a town now long gone. There are superb collections of early photographs; Mr Valentine of postcard fame did not neglect the topography and iconography of his own city, and more recent photographers have done full justice to Dundee and its magnificent surroundings.

This book is not another history: it attempts to present Dundee through the medium of local names, which are on everybody's lips but whose origin and significance are largely unknown or forgotten. It is not designed to be read from beginning to end, but offers a browse amidst Dundee's history and geography, with the emphasis on the city that many of us knew and loved but which disappeared forever in the 1970s.

Dundee has come in for more derogatory comment than practically any other Scottish city: Dr Johnson, en route for the Western Isles in 1773, stopped in the town but found in it 'nothing remarkable'; in more recent times Hugh MacDiarmid saw it as 'a grim monument of man's inhumanity to man' and James Cameron wrote of 'its brutal melancholy, its facade of of unparalleled charmlessness, its absence of grace so total that it was almost a thing of wonder'. Some of this criticism was no doubt justified, and the situation was not improved by the tearing-down of the remnants of the mediaeval city in the 1960s—something that would probably not have happened elsewhere and would certainly not occur today. In the years immediately following, Dundee seemed to lose its self-confidence: the old city of tramcars, jute-mills and marmalade factories had gone, and the industrial estates on the perimeter had failed to produce the expected revival. One might be tempted to say that Dundee is a City of Lost Opportunities, and there are

1

many who are disappointed by the recent riverside developments, which do nothing to dispel this notion. 'City of Discovery' is an ingenious promotional slogan, but is meaningless unless it is accompanied by self-discovery and self-awareness on the part of all Dundee's citizens; fortunately there are strong indications of a resolution on the part of the authorities to avoid repetition of past mistakes and to re-awaken a pride in civic achievements.

Reference has already been made to the pictorial histories of Dundee. This book is without illustrations—deliberately so, for its basis is names, which conjure up their own images. Many Dundee names are of a highly picturesque nature: and modern illustrations of such places as Meadowside, Springfield and Lilybank would merely destroy the illusion. These names were at the time of their coinage descriptive of a landscape which has changed beyond recognition. Other names such as Anchor Lane and Baffin Street recall something of the city's seafaring past; Baltic Street reminds us of former trading connections, while Peep o' Day Lane still has power to excite all but the deadest imagination.

It has to be said however that most Dundee place-names are what we would expect of the Dundonians who coined them—straightforward, down-to-earth and unpretentious. Take the number of suburbs and streets ending with the word 'field': **Maryfield**, Whitfield ('white field'), Downfield ('lower field'), Springfield ('field of the water source'), Marchfield ('boundary field'), Westfield—these would all have been 'greenfield sites' before they were at various times developed. Bellfield and Janefield seem to embody personal names.

Even commoner is the ending '-town'. In Scots parlance the term *toun* indicated part of an estate occupied by a number of farmers as co-tenants; later it came to mean the houses occupied by the farming families; later still the word tended to mean a village. (Side by side with this usage, a sixteenth-century Scot could refer to the Holy City as 'the toun o' Rome'.) In place-names toun, town and ton almost always have this landholding connotation: Maxwelltown would mean the urban estate of the Maxwells (see below). Several other examples of this type of place-name can be found in Dundee—Wallacetown is named after its proprietor (probably not *the* Wallace, but see **Wallace**); so are Charleston and **Clepington**; Hilltown is named for its situation but was formerly known as Rotten Row (probably meaning 'rat-infested'); Kirkton would be a settlement which grew up around a rural church. Place-names ending in -ton, toun and town probably date from the fourteenth century.

The suffix '-shade' (meaning 'division' as in 'watershed') indicates a somewhat larger landholding than 'field'; it crops up in Blackshade and

Chapelshade. The suffix '-croft' is also found, as in Blackscroft. Even more instructive is the suffix 'bank'. The geomorphology of much of the Dundee area is clearly indicated by some of the street-names. Hillbank, Forebank, Bonnybank, Lilybank and Rosebank (such lovely names!) must all refer to the terracing of the ground, the terrain being steeply sloping. Note however that the term 'terrace' in the more recent street names is a genteel Victorian concoction, usually descriptive of nothing in particular (although places such as Dudhope Terrace and Maryfield Terrace were probably built on artificially terraced land). Albany Terrace, along with Richmond Terrace and Windsor Street illustrate a passing fascination with the titles of royal dukedoms and are evidence of a desire to give suitably prestigious names to these new residential streets (which date from round about the 1870s).

A new council housing scheme at Kings Cross in the 1920s adopted for its street-names some of the Angus glens, including Glenprosen, Glenmarkie, Glenogil, Glenesk, Glenisla and Glenmoy; not a bad idea, but when they ran out of Angus glens, they had to stray as far afield as Glen Truim and Glen Affric. (A much older street is Glenagnes Road; its name was that of a former mansion in the Blackness Road area, and sounds as if it had been made up to celebrate a now-forgotten lady).

Sometimes officialdom decides that the names of new streets are to comprise a group of similar-sounding words, as happened in some of the newer municipal housing schemes (see **Fintry**); and the effect can appear contrived. By and large, the more modern one gets the less meaningful and relevant do the place-names become (e.g. Derwent Avenue or Hebrides Drive); but honourable exceptions are Claverhouse Road and Gotterstone Drive.

One of the most intriguing group of Dundee street-names is to be found in the Maxwelltown district, once well-known as the locus of Grimonds' carpet factory but now hidden away between Wellington Street and the Hilltown. (Its very name has disappeared from the street-maps, except for Maxwelltown Tower in Ann Street). The Maxwell family settled at Tealing around 1240 and for the next 500 years was one of the most notable in Angus. They owned property in the Hilltown until 1780, when David Maxwell, last of the Tealing lairds, gave off his Dundee estates in building lots. Nothing remains of the Maxwell town-house or of its environs, but his name, or rather those of his family, are commemorated in several of the surrounding streets. The feuing-plan drawn up by Maxwell stipulated that the new streets should be called Ann Street, Eliza Street, George Street, Alexander Street, Elizabeth Street and William Street—believed to be names of David Maxwell's numerous sons and daughters.

3

If you glance at a Dundee street directory you will notice the number of entries beginning with the syllable 'Bal-'; there are four full pages of them, and the reason for this profusion is that *bal* is a reduction of the Gaelic word *baile* meaning a town or village (sometimes just a feudal holding); the word is related to our 'bailie', a municipal officer, and comes ultimately from the Latin *ballium*, an enclosure. The area between the city and the Sidlaws is particularly rich in *bal-* place-names; and the nomenclature of a large number of Dundee streets is taken from surrounding farms and estates, some of them later becoming suburbs. There are no less than thirty-nine different *bal* places referred to in the street directory, mostly names of surrounding villages and farms, ranging from Balbeggie Street to Balunie Avenue.

Hardly less common are Dundee street-names which have the prefix 'Pit-': the most important thoroughfare of this type is Pitkerro Road—other examples are Pitairlie, Pitalpin, Pitcairn, Pitcaple, Pitcur, Pitempton, Pitfour, Pitlessie, Pitreavie and Pitroddie. Many of these again are taken from surrounding estates. *Pit* is an ancient Celtic word, cognate with Low Latin *petia*, and which passed into French and English as 'piece'. It appears to have been used in Pictish times as a semi-technical term to describe and classify land-holdings, and was taken over by Gaelic speakers who added their own qualifying epithet. In 'Pitkerro' the *pit* component can be taken to mean 'part' while *kerro* is a rendering of Gaelic *ceathramh* meaning 'quarter'; the whole name has the quite ordinary meaning of 'quarter-share' (and may be compared with the name Kirriemuir).

Pit is a much older term than *bal* (see above), and geographers have come up with the theory that places with the prefix *pit-* were settled at an earlier date than those with the prefix *bal-*. In effect, the early settlers bagged the best locations (the *pit-* ones, usually well-drained and south-facing) and left the others (the *bal-* ones) to later Gaelic-speaking incomers (this point is discussed under **Pitkerro**). All in all, Dundee street-names, as well as being interesting in themselves, give a very fair picture of the settlement of the pre-urban landscape.

Dundee also has its characteristic family-names, but of course none of these are exclusive to the city. Taking Scotland as a whole, the commonest surname by far is Smith, and the Dundee area is no different in this respect. The next five names in order of frequency hereabouts are Stewart, Robertson, Thomson, Brown and Anderson. There are no surprises in this: but in Fife the list would substitute Wilson for Robertson, and in the west of Scotland Campbell would come third.

As it happens, Thomson (sixth in the league for Scotland) is the only one of the top Scottish surnames that is discussed in this book. Of those surnames that figure in the text, Duncan comes in at Number 8 in the Scottish league, Walker at 15, Bell at 25, Wallace at 35, Low at 38, Gray at 39, Graham at 46, Fleming at 62 and Ogilvie at 98. (These figures, compiled by the Registrar General within the past decade, record 'occurrences'—presumably births, deaths and marriages—and the telephone directory might tell a different story). Other family names discussed in the text may be noteworthy rather than numerous—Baxter, Caird, Cox, Crichton, Draffen, Geddes, Gilroy, Grimond, Keiller, Morgan, Wedderburn and Wishart. But they are all indigenous to Dundee and certainly familiar to most citizens.

∗∗∗

A word is in order concerning the language of our city. The *Statistical Account of Scotland* (1793) notes, in respect of Dundee, that 'the language spoken by the inhabitants, has, from time immemorial, been the broad Scotch, that is English…with a peculiar provincial accent'. This observation was profoundly true at the time, and would still have been valid fifty years ago. Times have changed, and it is probably necessary on the threshold of the twenty-first century to remind ourselves of the phonological characteristics of the speech of our grandparents.

The characteristic Dundee sound is of course the substitution of the vowel 'e' for 'i'. This occurs most notably in the first person singular pronoun: so a Dundee émigré was heard to remark 'Eh've been awa fae Dundee that lang ye widnae ken whaur Eh come fae'. But of course the identical vowel sound appears also in polysyllabic words such as 'modernise' and 'recognise' (where the 'g' is silent).

More subtle perhaps is the frequent absence of any distinction between long and short vowels, or (more accurately) their idiosyncratic employment. 'Stalk' and 'stock' are pronounced the same, as are 'pauper' and 'popper'. The long English 'ae' sound becomes so short as to be almost inaudible: 'face' comes out as something like 'fiss'; and two Dundee lassies setting out on a long train journey from Tay Bridge station in the days of corridor trains and being unable to obtain a seat were heard to remark cheerfully 'Wull hae tae seh oan wir kisses' ('sit on our cases'). Conversely, English short vowels are often lengthened to produce the familiar Dundee drawl. A goods-vehicle is a 'law-rie', and a conventional expression of regret might be 'affy saw-rie'.

Dundee speech used to be renowned for its stridency, and it was often maintained that this was because the mill-workers (mainly women) had to contrive to make themselves heard over the hum of the machinery and the clack-clack of the shuttles; this, it is alleged, permanently affected Dundee vocal mechanisms and speech-patterns—and it may well be true. But a similar phenomenon is to be heard in many other non-industrial communities: Italian peasant women yacking at the market sound (at a distance) remarkably like the Dundee wifies of bygone days.

The glottal stop is another noticeable characteristic, but again Dundee is little different from other Scottish cities in this respect. The man who announced that his name was 'Pa''erson—spelt wi' twa t's' was a Fifer and not a Dundonian. But it was a Dundee laddie who, having enlisted in the Black Watch in 1916, felt very far from home while consuming his rations in a transit camp; he was considerably cheered by a loud voice from down the table which exclaimed 'Pass the bu''er! Eh come fae Dundee an' Eh like ma nourishment'.

In the days before we all became so frightfully cosmopolitan and laid-back, it could have been said that Dundee speech reflected in some measure the character of the speaker—straightforward, down-to-earth—brusque, if you like. Charm offensives, an unknown thing in this part of the world, would have been the subject of derision. Effusiveness in accepting a kindness was not common in Dundee speech; whether it might involve the offer of a 'wee hauf' or a free trip to the Bahamas, the acceptance-formula would be a simple 'Eh widnae mind'. On the other hand, disapproval of a situation would evoke more vehemence, as 'Eh couldnae be annoyed wi' thon'.

Conversations of a less than amicable nature tended to open with the monosyllable 'Here!' (probably an abbreviation of 'Look here!', but sounding even more peremptory and aggressive). A reminder of an overdue loan might begin 'Here, you're owe me fehv boab'. More seriously, 'Here, thon's meh lassie you're dancin wi''. The radical nature of local society will be touched on later in the book; it was ever-present in Dundee discourse, and the belief that 'Jack's as good as his master' was widely held (with more than a little justification), along with the idea that the term 'gentleman' could be applied to anyone, especially to oneself. The story goes that one day the telephone rang in the Police HQ in Bell Street and a voice announced: 'This is a gen'leman fae Lochee speakin'. Some **** has stolen meh ******* bike'.

These comments on our vernacular may of course apply to other Scottish dialects; and in any event the book's various representations of Dundee usage of half a century ago are set forth in a spirit of affectionate recollection and an awareness that Standard English continues and will continue to make huge inroads into the speech of all but the oldest and most stubborn of Scots folk.

Abertay

Aber is a very common prefix in Scottish place-names; it always refers to a river-mouth or to a confluence, and the *locus classicus* is Aberdeen—'mouth of the Don'. In our region a familiar example is Arbroath, of old *Aberbroth*, meaning 'the mouth of the Brothock burn'. Examples of *aber* meaning confluence include Aberargie (the River Farg and the Earn), Abernethy (the Nethy burn and the Earn), Aberuchil (the Ruchill Water and the Earn). So Abertay would seem from the linguistic point of view to be a genuine name referring to the mouth of Dundee's river.

But the first caveat is that Dundee is not of course situated at the mouth of the Tay: that distinction would belong to somewhere like Monifieth or even Buddon Ness. If you look eastwards from the Tay Bridge at low tide the bar of theTay is clearly visible; and to most of us who were brought up in Dundee over fifty years ago, the name Abertay would have meant the Abertay Sands and the Abertay lightship.

The name Abertay has for many years had a great appeal, and was adopted by several streets, properties and businesses in Broughty Ferry and Monifieth, including two guest houses and a golf club. It seems an appropriate enough name for these down-river establishments. Slightly more dubious is its adoption by a historical society founded in Dundee in 1947 in an attempt to revive the writing and publication of scholarly work on local history: although no study of Dundee can now be undertaken without extensive reference to the publications of the Abertay Historical Society, the name in such a context seems to lack a secure historical basis. And to those of the older generation for whom the name is inescapably associated with sand, mud and danger, Abertay seems perhaps an odd choice of name for Dundee's second university, although of course the symbolism provided by the association of the name with a lightship would be entirely appropriate. (The University of Abertay Dundee was formerly the Technical College, opened in Bell Street in 1911; the 'Tech', originally founded with the aid of benefactions from Sir David **Baxter** and Sir William Ogilvy **Dalgleish**, attained university status in 1992).

It is perhaps unfortunate that alphabetic selection places Abertay as the first name in this book; for despite its respectable credentials it seems to be a modern coinage, not found in any of the old records. The map of 1880 shows a property in Broughty Ferry, to the south of the Monifieth Road (then unbuilt on) with the name Abertay: this appears to be the first time the name was applied to dry land. The name may have been used somewhat earlier in connection with the sandbank off Tayport, although the map of 1827 describes the area simply as 'Mouth of Tay'. What does this matter?

7

Simply that if Abertay is indeed an invented name, it differs from other *aber* names such as Abernyte, recorded in the fourteenth century and having evolved from a simple geographical description of the confluence of two obscure rivulets in the braes of the Carse. And of course it makes Abertay that much less interesting as a historical onomastic specimen.

Airlie

In the early fifteenth century Sir Walter Ogilvie, a descendant of the earls of Angus and the chief of his clan, built the tower of Airlie by the side of a deep gorge through which runs the river Isla. The name Airlie is thought to derive from the Pictish words *ar ol*, meaning 'on the ravine', than which nothing could be more appropriate. Sir Walter's grandson was created Lord Ogilvie of Airlie in 1491, and a century and a half later his heir became the first earl of Airlie.

The Ogilvies of Airlie are the foremost landed family of Angus, and as such have played a significant part in the history of Dundee. Most of the county nobles had their town house; and that of the Ogilvies was 'Airly Lodge', lying between the Perth Road and the Hawkhill. The access to the property was by a road leading north from the Seabraes, known nowadays as Airlie Place. The northern part of the estate, where the mansion was probably sited, is now occupied by Airlie Hall, part of the University of Dundee.

The ancestral Angus lands gave their name to the parish of Airlie, which includes the old castle of Airlie and such places as the Kirkton of Airlie and the Den of Airlie. This latter, which included Reekie Linn and the Slug of Auchrannie, used to be a noted beauty spot, and a favourite destination for outings from Dundee. If it is less frequented nowadays it is possibly because stately homes and theme parks (with their attendant gift-shops and tearooms) have taken over in public affection.

Another Airlie property in or near Dundee was known as 'Peep o' Day'; it belonged to the Hon. Walter Ogilvie of Clova, who became the sixth titular earl of Airlie (the earldom having been attainted after the '45). His home was at Balnaboth in Glen Prosen, but Peep o' Day mansion was his town residence, built probably in the 1760s. Its location can be determined by the present Peep o' Day Lane, the mansion having been obliterated when the gas works were built in Dock Street later in the nineteenth century. It is not known why this name was chosen for the property; it seems to have been a catch-phrase descriptive of the first light of dawn. Difficult to imagine now that this aristocratic dwelling on the seashore would have had an uninterrupted view up and down the estuary. Peep o' Day was a haunt of the young Mary Wollstonecraft Godwin, who spent a year (1813-14) with the neighbouring Baxters in Broughty Ferry Road, where she began her famous novel *Frankenstein*, only months before her romantic elopement with the poet Shelley. Peep o' Day Lane is all that remains as a memorial of the estate and of Mary's stay in Dundee.

The lands of Airlie included the Loch of Lintrathen, and it was through the good offices of the 8th earl of Airlie that the perennial problem of the city's water supply was finally solved; in 1875 the earl was made a freeman 'in testimony of the Council's approbation of the cordial and equitable way in which he granted a supply of water from Lintrathen to the Town of Dundee'. The involvement of the 8th earl in Dundee's financial affairs was however speculative as well as charitable: he was a successful breeder of Aberdeen Angus cattle, and became chairman of the Prairie Cattle Company, a large public firm which was formed in 1880 in order to undertake cattle ranching in Texas. The earl's sudden death a year later preceded the collapse of this American investment venture, among many others. The noble lord had earlier pursued several different undertakings in the USA, and if any future historian should wonder why there is a township of Airlie in America, this is the connection; Airlie, Oregon, is probably by now several hundred times larger than the Kirkton in Angus.

Representatives of other branches of the house of Airlie have left their mark on Dundee, and of course there have been many untitled Ogilvie clansmen who have contributed to Dundee's story. One such was David Ogilvie, a founder member of the firm of Malcolm, Ogilvie and Co. Ltd (1851), still a big name in textiles in the city. The firm was active in building houses for its workers; Ogilvie Street was named after one of the factories in the Dens area, and Ogilvie Church presumably took its name from the street.

Albert

In some ways the Prince Consort is even better represented in Dundee's place-nomenclature than is his Queen (see **Victoria**). The Albert Institute was built in 1865-7 as part of a nationwide desire to share in the Queen's sense of loss at the death in 1861 of her beloved and high-minded husband; it also coincided with a wish on the part of the members of Dundee's emergent business class to acquire a visible symbol of their participation in the current cultural renaissance. The Albert Institute is Dundee's lasting memorial to the Victorian era, although since 1984 it has been known as 'the McManus Galleries' in memory of a former Lord Provost.

The original Institute, which consisted only of what is now the western wing with its grand horseshoe staircase (the central portion and eastern wing having been added later in the century) was intended as a cultural and educational establishment with lecture rooms and galleries; its opening was designed to coincide with the visit of the British Association to the city. Designed by Sir George Gilbert Scott, it is in the Gothic style so popular at the time and although not so stunning as his later design for Glasgow University's Gilmorehill, it fits in well with its surroundings. The city was going through one of its periods of near-bankruptcy at the time, and the building was financed by a private company headed by the **Baxter** family.

By the end of the nineteenth century the Institute had lost some of its educational purpose and sense of direction; it became the home of the city's higgledy-piggledy museum and also housed a somewhat undistinguished art collection, largely of the 'every-picture-tells-a-story' variety. (Both museum and gallery have been completely transformed in recent years, and deserve not one, but frequent and regular visits). The Institute also housed the central municipal lending library, but its chief asset was a magnificent and palatial chamber on the first floor, officially known as the Albert Hall, but later becoming a reference library (in popular parlance 'the Ref'). Situated as it was in the very centre of the town, the Ref was the haunt alike of schoolchildren in search of information, students seeking peace and quiet, and pensioners intent on reading the newspapers or just having a comfortable snooze. Indeed in the days before distance learning, this was the place where ordinary people could gain an education which had previously been denied to them; and usually every seat in the room was taken. The peaceful nature of the place had been interrupted in 1914, when the Ref was used as a recruiting depot where enlisting soldiers underwent medical and other forms of examination, part of the room being screened off for the purpose.

It is difficult to view the transfer of the library to Wellgate in 1978 as anything other than a great loss; one regrettable consequence was the abandonment of the horseshoe staircase in Albert Square as the main entrance, and its transfer to the ground floor on the north side. One used to issue from the reference library and stand at the top of the stone steps with a sense of being in the heart of a great and culturally-minded city—a feeling which the Wellgate signally fails to engender.

Unfortunately Albert Square has been to some extent spoiled by incessant and noisome traffic and will not come into its own until the whole area has been pedestrianised. The rest of the architecture of the square is largely of a piece with the Institute, and includes the Royal Exchange, unfortunately deprived of an intended tower due to the inadequacy of the foundations (see **Meadows**). Also to be regretted is the disappearance in 1968 of the Venetian-palatial Eastern Club which graced the south side of the square.

Albert Street, Prince's Street (the original spelling) and the now obscure Queen Street (which leads from Cowgate to Seagate) are all in the same area of the town, and their names might seem to be due to the same burst of monarchical fervour which also produced Albert Road in Broughty Ferry. But although Albert Street is indeed named after the Prince Consort and would seem to be a sort of south-easterly companion to Victoria Road, the name of King Street (forming part of the same thoroughfare) must give the lie to such a notion: King Street, formerly known as King's Road, was named in connection with an infirmary which was built there in 1798 (see **DRI**), and was given the royal title by the reigning monarch, George III— so the reference is to him. Queen Street will refer to his consort Charlotte, and Princes Street (to give the modern spelling) to his son, later Prince Regent and eventually George IV. To complete the picture, Carolina Port, later to become the site of a generating station, must be for the latter's unfortunate wife.

The Kingsway, Dundee's indispensable outer ring road, was the dream-child of James Thomson, the City engineer who was responsible for the initial design of the Caird Hall as well as of some superior muncipal housing. The Kingsway, originally to be a wide, tree-lined avenue, was a long time in the planning and construction. For some years after its completion it marked the effective perimeter of the city, and the spread of housing beyond it is mainly post-1945; more recently the creation of new industrial estates has largely obliterated this concept. The name Kingsway, devised during the planning stage, was meant to commemorate the current monarch, Edward VII, although the actual completion was in the reign of Victoria and Albert's grandson George V.

Angus

One of the benefits of the recent (1996) reorganisation of local government administration in Scotland is that Dundee ceases to be in Tayside and becomes once again the principal town of Angus. Tayside, which one hopes will disappear from the future map of Scotland, was always a feeble appellation—more appropriate to a but-and-ben in Birnam or Grandtully than to a great region. Angus on the other hand is a splendid name, which recalls more than a thousand years of history. It originated as the Celtic personal name Aonghus, consisting of the elements *aon* (one) and *gus* (choice), and gained great cachet from being the name of an early Irish prince. The first Angus was one of the three sons of Erc, high king of Ireland; the *Cenel nOengusa* ('kindred of Angus') were one of the principal peoples of the Kingdom of Dalriada (see under **Gowrie**), and according to Irish legend they settled the lands between Tay and Dee. That is one story (unverifiable and perhaps unlikely) of how the district of Angus got its name.

Moving on to surer historical ground, Angus as a place-name denoted a unit of the Pictish confederation that preceded the mediaeval kingdom of Scotland, and it is more probable that the derivation of the name is from *Oengus* (Angus), son of Fergus, over-king of Pictland. The district of Angus was of great strategic importance, lying as it did on the principal route between south and north. It was through these lands that the Roman legions marched to do battle at Mons Graupius; along the same route in AD 685 came the Northumbrian invaders, fortunately for Scotland to be checked at the battle of Nectansmere.

In the mediaeval period Angus was governed by a *mormaer* ('great steward') and some hundred years later it became an earldom. The first earl was Gillebride, progenitor of the clan Ogilvie, whose chiefs became hereditary sheriffs of the area during the fourteenth century. The term Angus therefore came to describe a shire as well as an earldom—but not until the lapse of several centuries; for some reason Forfarshire, the title of the mediaeval sheriffdom, became the preferred name of the county, with Angus as a (largely unused) alternative. It was increasingly felt however that this was an aberration and a slight to Dundee, and the name reverted to Angus in 1928.

The family name of the earls was not of course Angus, but Umfraville (a Northumbrian surname which mercifully became obsolete in Scotland in the later middle ages); the Umfraville earls fell from favour, one of them having acted traitorously as Governor of Dundee during the Wars of Independence. In 1329 Robert the Bruce conferred the earldom on a Stewart kinsman, the widow of one of whose descendants re-married with a Douglas. The dukedom of Douglas became conjoined with the earldom of Angus, but both titles lapsed in the mid-eighteenth century. (The combined title was by some curious quirk revived with the creation of the unimaginative housing scheme of Douglas and Angus—the 'terrible twins' of the Christmas pantomimes—but few of the inhabitants can be aware of the august origin of the nomenclature.)

From being a forename, Angus soon gained wide currency as a surname (its Gaelic equivalent is MacInnes and in Ireland it is Hennessy). But it is not commemorated in any street or indeed any public institution in the city; it figures in the title of many small businesses, but less so in Dundee than in places like Forfar and Carnoustie—perhaps an indication that Dundee has related less well with its hinterland than has, say, Aberdeen. Although the Angus Hotel may once have provided a useful service to Dundee's social and commercial life, one struggles to find something kind to say about the complex of 1960s buildings of which it was the centrepiece.

Armitstead

All the early records of the burgh were destroyed when Dundee was ravaged by the English soldiery in the mid-sixteenth century. In 1581 the then Town Clerk (see **Wedderburn**) resolved to compile a Roll of Burgesses, reconstructing the more recent records from his own and the communal memory. The result of his labours became known as the Lockit Buik, and complete records have been maintained to the present day. The right of admission to the Roll was always for some specific cause, and involved taking the Burgess Oath of loyalty to sovereign and country. The lucky person thereupon became a freeman of the burgh (or freewoman, but there were very few of them).

The first name to appear is John Scrymgeour, Constable of Dundee in 1513 (see **Scrimgeour**), and the list of honorary citizens, which includes Viscount Duncan (see **Camperdown**) and Prince **Albert**, stretches down to the present day. One of the less obvious inclusions is the name of George Armitstead in 1854.

Armitstead was the son of a Yorkshireman, born in Russia and educated in Germany. At the time of his marriage to one of the Baxter daughters (see **Baxter**), he was a merchant in Archangel. To consolidate his naturalised status, the influential Baxters arranged for his election to Parliament. This could be achieved only with some difficulty, for Armitstead's command of English was not impressive. He stood (as a Liberal, but a conservative one) against Sir John Ogilvy of **Baldovan** in 1857, on an anti-Catholic ticket, or, as his supporters put it, as 'an upholder of the broad principles of Civil and Religious Freedom'. They commissioned a full-length portrait of him and presented it to Mrs Armitstead the following year; it is rather good, in fact, and now occupies a prominent place in the Albert Hall of the McManus Galleries. Although Armitstead was defeated in 1857 he had become recognised as 'an upright, honourable and public-spirited citizen'; the city took him to its heart, and despite failing health he was elected unopposed in 1868 when Dundee became a two-member constituency.

Armitstead seems to have recovered his health, for he again served as MP for Dundee between 1880 and 1885. When his close friend Gladstone died in 1898 Armitstead acted as a pall-bearer at the funeral of the Grand Old Man.

His benevolence continued, with princely donations to the new University College (which of course was largely a Baxter foundation) and other benefactions in the area of child welfare (now represented by a Child Development Centre in Broughty Ferry). He continued to reside in the palatial mansion which he had built on the western outskirts of the city (Duncarse, Perth Road) until his death in 1915.

The name Armitstead comes from the north-west of England and simply means 'hermitage'. The Armitstead Lectures are a Dundee institution, and Armitstead has in effect become a Dundee name—this despite the fact that not one citizen in a thousand could nowadays tell you who the man was. There may be some excuse for this, because the contemporary records are curiously reticent about this benevolent peer, and he does not figure in the *Dictionary of National Biography*. Although for a time his immediate descendants played some part in Dundee's affairs, there appear to be no Armitsteads left in Scotland (although there are one or two Armisteads, an even rarer form of the name). Curious, but there is surely an innocent explanation.

Baldovan

Baldovan was the name of an estate near Strathmartine, and when in the 1830s it was decided that Dundee should expand to the north, Baldovan village was to be the nucleus of the new development. The Hilltown was extended under the name of Strathmartine Road, but the new suburb acquired the name of Downfield. So the name Baldovan survived in the Dundee vocabulary as that of a mill on the Dighty, a corrective institution and a former tram terminus; nowadays it will be familiar as the name of a busy street leading from Downfield to Strathmartine Hospital.

Baldovan was one of the numerous properties around Dundee possessed by the **Scrymgeour** family; it was in their hands in the early seventeenth century, and passed to the Fife family of Nairne about 1680. David Wedderburn was proprietor in 1710, by which time the estate had come to be known as 'The Bank'; thirty years later a Dr Walter Tullideph, retired nabob and brother of the redoubtable Thomas, Principal of St Leonard's College, St Andrews, bought the two estates of Baldovan and **Balgay**. Some of these names are commemorated in thoroughfares in the area: Tullideph Road, Street and Place are in what was the Balgay estate, while Bank Avenue in Downfield perpetuates the transient name of the Baldovan estate.

A proposal to re-name Baldovan House as 'Tullideph Hall' having failed to catch on, the property passed in the late-eighteenth century to the Ogilvys of Inverquharity under the name by which it is still known. As recently as fifteen years ago, a useful architectural guide to Dundee was able to describe

Baldovan House as 'a large three-storey classical mansion fronted by a triumphal stairway and arch through which one entered into a *piano nobile* on the first-floor level'. There was talk at that time of converting the empty mansion into a hotel; but now alas Baldovan House is roofless and sightless, its lawns covered with debris and rubbish, its borders overgrown with willowherb and other rank weeds. Only the odd surviving azalea adds a splash of spring colour to the scene, and wild hyacinths (*anglice* bluebells) brighten the woodland. The winding drive still provides a pleasant walk, and a reminder that Baldovan and its rolling parkland could have become a civic amenity as attractive in its own way as **Camperdown**.

Sir John Ogilvy of Baldovan, 9th baronet of Inverquharity and an aristocratic Whig of the better type, was MP for Dundee for sixteen years and a noted public benefactor. It was through his generosity and that of his wife Lady Jane that in 1852 the nearby Baldovan Institute was built 'for helpless and afflicted patients'; originally designated as Baldovan Asylum 'for Imbecile and Idiot Children', it was brought under NHS control in 1948 as Strathmartine Hospital, now very greatly extended.

The name Baldovan comes from the Gaelic words *baile domhain* and means something like 'deep settlement' or (in context) 'farm in the hollow', no doubt in reference to the deep dell of the **Dighty** at this point. Only two letters differentiate the name Baldovan from Baldovie which lies three and a half miles to the east. Baldovie is or was a hamlet with a toll-house on the B978 to Kellas and Letham (it has more or less attached itself to the eastern extremity of Whitfield), and the name scarcely impinged on the Dundee consciousness. But the new Baldovie Road is of arterial quality, linking Arbroath Road with the northern suburbs, and the name has also been adopted by the motor trade. There is probably no etymological connection between the two names, but the similarity in appearance might have led to some confusion, were it not that the local pronunciation gives 'Balduvvan' for the one and 'Baldoavie' for the other.

Balgay

Reference is made in the **Introduction** to the huge number of Dundee names beginning with the syllable *bal-* : Balgay is one such, being until the nineteenth century a rural property situated on a hill-slope to the west of the town. The name is probably from *baile gaoithe*—'windy place'—and may be compared with Milngavie near Glasgow.

Balgay Hill as seen from the road bridge has pleasing contours, and the whole area was once known for its scenic beauty. The *First Statistical Account of Scotland* (1793) describes it in these terms: 'The valley, where the stream of Balgay runs, is exceedingly beautiful; and few situations can be conceived more delightful, than those of the castle of Dudhope, and the house of Logie to the north of the valley; of the house of Balgay at its western extremity; or of Blackness on the ridge on the south of it'. Balgay House dates from the 1760s, and was one of the larger 'laird's hooses' in the area; a century later it was incorporated into the block which comprises the Royal Victoria Hospital, and the adjoining Victoria Park was created from its former 'pleasance'.

It is difficult to determine the extent of the estate of Balgay, and the old maps are not of much help in distinguishing it from the larger estate of **Blackness**. The fact that the present City Road was formerly named 'Balgay Street' may indicate that the estate stretched further east than one might have supposed. And the *Statistical Account* refers to the 'coast at Balgay' as being 'perpendicular', presumably with reference to the escarpment at Harris Academy which marked the shoreline before systematic land reclamation created **Riverside** Drive.

The crowning glory of Balgay is of course its hill, acquired by the city in 1871 as a 'place of recreation'. Attractively wooded at the summit, the hill provides one of the most picturesque municipal parks in Scotland, with well-preserved natural features including rocky ravine, groves and shrubberies. Illustrations from the last century show a bare summit with oaks and Scots pines on the upper slopes; although housing has encroached to some extent, the prospect is still pleasing.

Balgay Park also houses the famous Mills Observatory, the only one in the United Kingdom designed for popular use and instruction. John Mills was a nineteenth-century Dundee industrialist with a penchant for astronomy who owned a private observatory on the slopes of the **Law**; he left his considerable fortune for the provision of a public observatory 'suitable for the study of the wonder and beauty of the works of God in creation'. The observatory (originally intended for the summit of the Law, a plan pre-empted by the erection of the war memorial) opened in 1935; in more recent years it achieved, in collaboration with the Astronomy Department of St Andrews University, an improvement in its access and viewing facilities. The construction of the buildings gave much-needed employment in the depressed 30s, but the benefits of the observatory itself have been even more long-lasting.

The associations of the name Balgay however are not exclusively with scenic beauty and stellar observation. Let us not forget Balgay Works in Lower Pleasance, between Brook Street and Lochee Road, truly one of the most depressing parts of the city's former industrial heart. At one time

Balgay Works employed more jute workers than any other mill in Dundee. Now all is dereliction.

Balgillo

This is one of the older names in the Dundee district; it probably comes from the Gaelic *baile gille-each*—literally 'horse-servant's stead'. Nowadays one thinks of Balgillo Road, which runs from the Claypotts roundabout in the west to Barnhill in the east, and which for most of its length represents the northern boundary of that section of the city. To the south of the road lies a large private housing estate, one of those developed in the 1960s to cater for the needs of Dundee's expanding middle class.

In earlier times the lands of Balgillo had been an estate in a different sense, comprising a large part of the present Broughty Ferry, excluding West Ferry and Barnhill. Broughty Castle when it was acquired by Lord Gray at the end of the fifteenth century (see **Broughty**) consisted only of a tower on a rock; his purchase of the Balgillo lands in 1499 gave the castle a landward estate, with hamlets and farms to provision it. The estate preserved its identity until the late nineteenth century, with the mansion-house of Balgillo situated somewhere to the east of the bend in the present Claypotts Road.

It is the earlier history of Balgillo which is possibly most interesting. Ancient fortifications were discovered on Balgillo Hill when the foundations of Castleroy were being dug; they included traces of a former encampment (at one time thought to be Roman) along with human remains and fragments of weaponry. The name of Camphill Road is there to remind us. More than a millennium later it was from Balgillo Hill that an invading English force mounted its siege of Broughty Castle, and its alternative name of Forthill refers to this event, which took place in 1547. The English invasion was part of a dynastic plan to contrive a marriage between the young heir of Henry VIII and the infant Mary Queen of Scots and thus secure a union of the two kingdoms (or more accurately an English takeover of Scotland); it came to nothing, but necessitated the removal of the young princess to the continent for protection at the French court. More importantly it involved the almost total evacuation of Dundee's citizenry and the destruction of much of the town.

Attempts by the Scots during the next three years to recapture the strategic fortress of Broughty were made more difficult by the strength of the English fortifications at Balgillo, only half a mile away, and by the large size of its garrison. In February 1550 however the Regent Arran, with a considerable force, aided by a French contingent, laid siege to Balgillo fort. After a heavy artillery bombardment and a successful assault, which resulted in many English casualties, the fort was cut off from Broughty Castle; the next day the garrison of the Castle surrendered.

There are no traces remaining of the English fort on the hill, and since it has long since become a built-up area (under the name of Forthill) none are likely to be uncovered. Indeed Balgillo made a swift exit from the pages of Scotland's history; the estate was sold off in the mid-seventeenth century by the Gray family, who had run into financial difficulties, and for a period until the 1950s the name figured on the map only in with reference to East Balgillo farm (a neighbour of Barnhill farm). Balgillo is now a comfortable residential area with no untidy gardens or mortgage payments in arrears; respectability reigns.

Ballumbie

In the far-off days of one's boyhood, when there was a race-course at Longhaugh and Whitfield was a little hamlet straggling along a country road, the city of Dundee lay well to the south of the Dighty valley. The relentless spread to the north-east has changed all this, and suburbia now stretches over the once pleasant fields. It is not known why most of the new streets off Berwick Drive have Lothian or Border names, such as Haddington Avenue and Coldstream Drive; but at least one of them retains a meaningful name, and that is Ballumbie Road.

Bal means a settlement or village or farm (see **Introduction**); Lumb was a personal name very common in the Lowlands in mediaeval times, and is now represented by the surnames Lamb and Lambie (the 'b' ought to be silent). So Ballumbie would mean something like 'Lambie's farm'. It is no doubt Ballumbie House, near Duntrune, that gives the road its name; but there is an older and more interesting place nearby. This is the fourteenth-century Ballumbie Castle, of which all that now remains are a curtain wall and two circular towers. Although the castle has been a ruin for centuries, and not much is known of its origin, it apparently belonged in the sixteenth century to a family called Lovell. Many stories were current about the lawless brigand, Henry Lovell of Ballumbie, who was the terror of the locality. At Monifieth, for example, he evicted the minister by burning down the manse, and his brutal treatment of tenants at West Ferry was the subject of a complaint to the Privy Council; his depredations on his neighbour at **Pitkerro** are mentioned under that heading.

There is perhaps some poetic justice in the circumstance that the castle of Ballumbie should, several centuries later, have been subjected to the same sort of vandalism as was practised by its own wicked lairds. Gang slogans cover the age-old walls, and the place is knee-deep in offensive

18

litter. Even worse is the adjoining ruin of Ballumbie House, a Victorian pile of no architectural distinction which succumbed some twenty years ago, apparently to the ravages of dry rot; the former grandeur of the property may be gauged by the imposing gateway of the huge walled garden, and by the winding woodland drive, some half a mile in length. The house is now a target for the destructive impulses of young Dundonians, and is also used by their elders as a dumping ground for assorted items of discarded household furniture. The whole scene is one of almost unimaginable dereliction and depression: the contrast with the neighbouring estates of pretty Pitkerro and functional Linlathen could hardly be more complete.

Baltic

Most of the names of Dundee's older streets were purely descriptive—like **Overgate** and **Seagate**—but Baltic Street seems to have been so named in a conscious attempt to recall the old days of the linen trade with Riga and other Baltic ports. Baltic Street was opened in 1840 to form an access from Meadowside to the Wellgate: it disappeared with the erection of the Wellgate Centre in 1977, and all that remains are a truncated lane and a block called Baltic Buildings. Nevertheless these names are a reminder of the importance of Dundee's trading concerns in the days before it became the nineteenth century Juteopolis.

Dundee's commercial links with Western Europe had begun as early as the thirteenth century and flourished for more than three hundred years before being interrupted by the disturbances of the civil wars of the seventeenth century.

The principal exports were sheepskins, wool, hides and agricultural produce, in exchange for timber, iron, tar, pitch, salt and wine. This had never become a highly organised system, but operated instead on an opportunistic basis, with continually changing trading-partners. In the eighteenth century wool was gradually replaced by flax as Dundee's chief imported raw material; the manufacture of linen introduced a new era, necessitating the construction of a larger harbour to provide for the rapidly expanding Baltic flax trade. Baltic hemp was greatly superior to Indian hemp, which was first introduced to Dundee in 1810; commercial links with German and Russian traders became quite extensive in the nineteenth century, establishing Dundee as a more cosmopolitan city than its popular image might suggest.

Prosperity came of course not from the fact of importing the raw fibre (which to some extent had also been grown locally) but with spinning it into yarn and making it into fine linen. This was the foundation of the **Baxter** fortunes; and linen continued to be Dundee's staple manufacture until jute came to replace flax around the time of the Crimean War in 1854, when tension between Britain and Russia had introduced uncertainty into trading relations.

Another trade of the pre-jute era was the manufacture of candles, carried out by one Joseph Sanderson in a street off the Seagate which came to be called Candle Lane. Sanderson styled himself in 1760 'tobacconist and candle-maker', but the connection between the two trades is far from obvious. The more relevant operation of soap-making was carried out by the same man in Soapwork Lane off Victoria Road. Sugar House Wynd, near the Cowgate, is a reminder of another of the town's cottage industries; Anchor Lane, off Henderson's Wynd, recalls its maritime past. The name of Horsewater Wynd, near the Scourin Burn, commemorates what was the city's only mode of transport until well into the present century.

Baxter

This is a very common Angus surname, the Scottish equivalent of the English name Baker; indeed there is a tradition that the Baxters of Forfar were hereditary bakers at the royal residence there. In Dundee the name has a particular resonance, due entirely to the phenomenal business success and philanthropy of one remarkable family.

Its first recorded member, John Baxter, came to Dundee in 1728 from the Angus hinterland and became a weaver; he prospered, and his name is to be found in the Burgess Roll of Dundee of 1777. His son was a flax spinner in the city and his grandson William established the family firm in 1807 with a flax mill on part of the site of the existing Dens works. William Baxter contrived to join the landowning classes with the acquisition of the estate of Balgavies (pronounced 'Balguise') near Forfar; in 1820 he assumed his four sons as partners in a spinning enterprise which first got off the ground when they bought the spinning mill at Glamis from the earl of Strathmore's factor. The firm, with the astonishing number of 600 employees at Glamis, and now able to spin its own yarn, had transferred its operations to Dundee, where the Dens burn provided the necessary motive power for a 15 h.p. spinning mill. Of the brothers, the most go-ahead was David, who was mainly responsible for major extensions to the Dens works; by this time the adoption of steam power made the mills less dependent on a water supply, and Lower Dens works was constructed in Princes Street, followed by a rebuilding of Upper Dens works. Sir David Baxter of Kilmaron (as he became, although the baronetcy died with him in 1872) amassed a vast fortune, partly through his own efforts and partly through delegation

20

of work to his engineer, Peter Carmichael, whose native ingenuity and forward-looking attitude made the Dens enterprise (in his own words) 'better than a gold mine'.

The Baxters led the field in the manufacture of linen. It was this firm who had made the sails for Nelson's *Victory*; and succeeding wars stimulated the demand for the Baxter textile products of flax and hemp. Wars were not lacking—Crimea in 1854, the Franco Prussian war of 1860 and the American Civil war in 1861—all these improved the firm's profits without adversely affecting the economic prosperity of the UK. But sail gave way to steam, and by the time of the 1914-18 war the boom was over; ten years later Baxter Brothers had been acquired by Low and Bonar and the great textile empire was no more. Lower Dens mill was demolished, and the Upper mill has recently been the subject of an imaginative and successful housing conversion.

The Baxters used typical nineteenth-century methods to enrich themselves, and it has never been denied that the social conditions in which their employees had to work were appalling. To meet the acute housing shortage in Dundee in the mid-nineteenth century the firm was forced to build property—for example in Lyon Street—which soon underwent subdivision to accommodate additional incoming workers; the result was dreadful overcrowding in filthy and insanitary conditions. Female labour was cheaper and more docile than male; and the introduction of double-loom working increased the already frantic pace of production. But the Baxters, despite their anti-trade union attitudes, were not the worst type of mill-owner, and schemes of welfare began to emerge. Although child labour was common there was an attempt to provide education, the first factory-school having been built in Dens Brae in 1840; Mary Slessor of Calabar was a 'half-timer' at Baxters mill during her girlhood. Donations to the workers of refreshment and reading rooms, model lodging houses and allotments, and the encouragement of temperance societies may sound like mere Victorian do-goodery—the addition of hypocrisy to exploitation. But the later members of the Baxter family, by now strong proponents of Liberal Unionism, had at heart the well-being of their workers; and the provision of schooling and transport (including a dedicated early-morning tramway service to the Dens works) was in the interests of welfare as well as efficiency.

The Baxter family is remembered in Dundee for philanthropy rather than capitalist exploitation, and their chief monument is Baxter Park. It was in 1863 that Sir David and his two sisters purchased a 35-acre chunk of the estate of **Craigie** and presented it to the inhabitants of Dundee as a recreation ground. While the park is still greatly enjoyed by the neighbouring inhabitants and their children, it is important to remember that in the 1860s it was still in the countryside; the Renaissance pavilion at the north end (designed by Joseph Paxton of Crystal Palace fame) was there for the purpose of sheltering visitors who in most cases had come from a distance. The pavilion once housed a statue of Sir David, paid for by public subscription; it was moved to the McManus Galleries (formerly the **Albert** Institute) and so escaped the attention of the mindless vandals who have all but destroyed the pavilion. (The trouble of course is that the park gates and railings had to be removed in 1939 in aid of the war effort, and since then there has been no means of excluding undesirables; there seems to be no answer to this problem, which has been exacerbated by a reduction in the number of 'parkies' on the beat and which is common to many public parks throughout the land).

The list of Sir David's other benefactions would include endowment of professorial chairs and university scholarships, and the building of convalescent homes, technical institutes and churches. Perhaps the most notable family benefaction however is that of Sir David's sister, Mary Ann Baxter of Balgavies, who, along with her relative John Boyd Baxter, in 1880 donated a large sum for the foundation of a University College in Dundee. After a century of fluctuating fortunes the University of Dundee is now firmly established in the international world of learning.

Beechwood

A lovely name for an unlovely place; if that seems too harsh, it may be remembered that Beechwood for a long time had the reputation of being one of Dundee's two problem areas (the other being Mid-Craigie) and these names still conjure up images of squalor without the charm of antiquity. But let us try to understand and not merely to judge.

Beechwood was no doubt a descriptive name at one time; Beechwood House had been built on the land that formed part of the large **Cox** estate which included Clement Park and Foggyley, and as the locus of one of the family homes it would have natural amenities apart from its beautiful setting on the northern heights of the city. In 1934 Beechwood was purchased by the corporation and the mansion demolished, as one of two locations for an extensive slum-clearance programme, the other being Mid-Craigie. (There is no need to be squeamish about this term: the various inter-war Housing Acts were quite specific about the need, with government subsidy, to decant whole populations from the overcrowded and depressed areas of the inner city). The new locations were carefully chosen, and the planning process was elaborate in the extreme: these were to be showpieces, and a five-man delegation selected from the Scottish Department of Health and the local authorities was sent to study council housing estates in Holland, Germany, Czechoslovakia, Austria and France. The final plans in respect of Dundee involved continuous tenement development around a rectangular plan, taking in an open courtyard on either side; new features were the inclusion of sun-balconies,internal staircases (to avoid the old concept of the 'closie') and ornamental brick facings. The plans were well executed and it seemed that the intention had been achieved of removing a social evil and of creating a new and attractive housing environment.

What went wrong? For a start, the tenants of the Mid-Craigie scheme were by 1937 petitioning the Corporation concerning the unmanageable costs of bussing themselves to work and their children to school; they complained, not unreasonably, about the distance from the shops and the lack of any recreational and social facilities. The Beechwood tenants had the same problems; and in addition the layout of the scheme, so impressive on the drawing-board, proved inconvenient and unattractive in practice. Add to that the fact that the sun seldom shone on the balconies, many of which were in any event used for domestic storage purposes. Bad planning produces adverse social conditions, leading to vandalism and poor maintenance by tenants; in time vacant houses become difficult to let—and you rapidly approach slum conditions of a more expensive type.

Beechwood and Mid-Craigie were innovative in their day, and their problems were those of peripheral development in hundreds of other cities in the United Kingdom. It would be reassuring to say that the lessons were duly learned and applied: but unfortunately similar mistakes were perpetrated in the creation of other subsequent schemes—Whitfield being a notable example. The result has been the necessity in recent years to repair and upgrade these estates, sometimes involving enormous expenditure in demolition and rebuilding. The prospects are now much better, and Beechwood may yet come to live up to the beautiful associations of its name.

Bell

Samuel Bell was born in Dundee in 1739 and was brought up to follow his father's trade of wright or joiner; but the young apprentice showed great skill in design as well as in construction, and developed an architectural practice which led in time to his appointment as the first City Architect. Bell perhaps never quite outgrew his tradesman's origins, and his building portfolio falls short of greatness; Dundee was not to achieve anything comparable to the New Town of Edinburgh which was being built at the time that Bell was operating; nevertheless he deserves wider recognition in his native city.

Bell's masterpiece is undoubtedly St Andrews church in the Cowgate; completed in 1772, this simple countrified building with its graceful steeple looks over the street which took its name from the church, and in its original semi-rural setting it must surely have justified the enthusiasm with which it was greeted on its completion. The environs have greatly changed with the erection of the Wellgate Centre, whose blank and brutal east wall dwarfs the 'pretty little country church' as it was described early in the nineteenth century. Nevertheless, St Andrews church still deserves contemplation by those who are looking for survivors of Dundee's lost architectural heritage.

One such loss was another Bell building, the elegant Trades Hall, which stood in front of the Clydesdale Bank in the High Street; it is familiar to antiquarians in the celebrated caricature of Dundee Town Council, done in the early nineteenth century and entitled 'The Executive'. No-one is really to blame for the demolition of this building in the 1870s, for it had been badly sited at the former market place which stood at the junction of the Seagate, and had to be removed from that incredibly cluttered area which was once the heart of the mediaeval city. Another Bell building, the Union Hall, which was in the Nethergate and faced the Trades Hall, was removed at the same time and for the same reasons. It is a pity that the Dundee planning authorities of the late eighteenth century did not have a more grandiose conception of civic development, so that these pleasant buildings might have survived to grace more appropriate locations.

The old Theatre Royal (see **Castle** Street) also occupied an inappropriate site, since it could never have been viewed from a distance exceeding twenty yards. The Morgan Tower (1794) in the Nethergate has a more open situation, and in consequence is better known to Dundonians; Bell may indeed have rebuilt it on the site of a late mediaeval structure. Across the road is a building, commonly accepted to have been designed by Bell, which in its way is the most interesting of all. It is Nethergate House, now occupied by a branch of the Clydesdale Bank but once the dwelling of Dundee's famous—or notorious—Provost (see **Riddoch**).

It would be pleasing to be able to record that Bell Street was named in honour of the worthy but unassuming Samuel; this would be incorrect, but the Riddoch connection is still there. During the turmoil of 1793, the 'Friends of Liberty', intent on obtaining the traditional and symbolic Tree of Liberty, stole a sapling from the grounds of Belmont House in Perth Road, owned by one Thomas Bell; the mob decorated it like a modern Christmas tree, and erected it at the Mercat Cross in the High Street.

There was much sympathy in Dundee with the radical movement, and after Riddoch had pacified the mob he considered that it would be preferable to return the tree to Belmont rather than further inflaming the populace by destroying it. Thus it was that the tree flourished for over a century until the widening of Perth Road necessitated its removal. Meanwhile Thomas Bell had founded the flax-spinning firm of Bell and Balfour and had been elevated to the provostship; he died in 1844, full of years and civic honours, and he it was who had named after him a street, dominated by the Sheriff Court, and later by the Police Headquarters and the cells (then called the Bridewell), and inescapably associated in the public mind with the workings of the law. A far cry, perhaps, from the libertarian tree which Provost Bell had unwittingly nurtured; and a pity that the name of the equally deserving Samuel Bell (no relation) is uncommemorated.

Blackness

The current street map of Dundee shows Blackness as being the area to the north of Perth Road, between Glamis Road and Farington Street, and this indeed was the location of the former Blackness tram terminus. But Blackness School, the Blackness Library and the Blackness Business Development Area all lie fully a mile to the east. So there might appear to be some doubt about the precise location of the area known historically as Blackness.

Originally the name Blackness referred to a 'ness' or headland of black rock to the east of the Magdalen Green. When the railway line was laid in the late nineteenth century it had to cross this (apparently anonymous) headland, which was thereupon named after the chairman of the Committee of the House of Lords responsible for the operation: he was Lord Buckingham, hence Buckingham Point, near the present marshalling yards. But the records show that the estate which was named after the 'black ness' occupied a large area to the west of this point. It was in the ownership of a Captain Henry Lyall in the sixteenth century; he contributed to the restoration of the transept of the city church which had been destroyed in 1548 by the Auld Enemy (England). In 1650 Sir Alexander **Wedderburn** acquired the lands, Charles II having restored him to the position of town clerk of the burgh. There used to be an ancient oak at Blackness said to have been planted by that monarch when on a visit to Sir Alexander.

The financial affairs of the Wedderburns having gone into decline, the estate and mansion were sold in 1743 to Alexander Hunter of Balskelly. In the latter part of the eighteenth century more than a hundred acres were feued by the Hunters as building lots. The *First Statistical Account* tells us that in 1772 there were no more than five or six houses between Blackness and the town boundary; but twenty years later, through the process of sub-feuing, there were at least 4,000 people in the district—a figure which had increased very considerably by the year 1900.

The Hunters were a well-known family in their day: in the National Gallery of Scotland there hangs an early Raeburn portrait (1788) of David Hunter of Blackness. The family retained the mansion of Blackness until the 1920s; there is now no trace whatever of the house, and the street-layout of the area has completely changed in the past century. But the old maps show Blackness House as being slightly to the north of the present Corso Street; and a late seventeenth-century drawing (admittedly neither detailed nor accurate) indicates that the lower part of the present Blackness Avenue was originally the approach to the mansion. So the estate of Black-ness (which stretched as far east as the present Tay Street) was in fact much nearer to the town centre than the name of the old tram routes would have us suppose.

Blackness Road used to be a busy thoroughfare, but with the odd feature that it petered out at the former city boundary with no outlet to the open country to the west. The development of the new road systems around Ninewells Hospital and Menzieshill have further detracted from the impor-tance which it formerly had. Blackness Road was a typical Dundee creation, starting at the slums near the West Port and ending at expensive houses with glorious views over the river. The lower end of the road was indeed one of Dundee's black spots; as the nineteenth-century gazetteer colour-fully points out, the old town 'occupies chiefly a stripe of ground along the base of an acclivity, and seems pent up by Dundee-law and Balgay-hill as if they were a pursuing foe urging it into the sea...' This was an accurate description of the terrain, and explained the gross overcrowding in parts of the old city, particularly around the foot of Blackness Road.

The ancient hovels gave place to industrial developments which were scarcely more salubrious, and a City Guide of 1873 describes 'the combi-nation of closely packed mills, and miserable unwholesome dwellings' on the site of what had once been the pleasance of Dudhope Castle. The area has recently undergone a change for the better, and from the junction of Blackness Road and Hawkhill you can now get a good impression of the situation of Dudhope Castle in relation to the mediaeval town.

Further changes will follow with the inception of a regional project headed by the Scottish Development Agency whose aim is to regenerate former industrial buildings or replace them with custom-built industrial units. A good example of the former can conveniently be seen at West

Marketgait, where the Tay Works has been developed to provide student accommodation and a new-style shopping complex; an indication of the way in which this part of Dundee is adapting to the post-jute era.

Broughty

In the days before the Tay road bridge a party of cyclists entered the city from the Forfar Road with the intention of crossing to Fife and then proceeding south. Unfamiliar with the city, they enquired of a Dundonian the way to the ferry: they were duly directed to Broughty Ferry. Since there is no way of distinguishing in the spoken word between 'the ferry', and 'The Ferry'; and since a native Dundonian would regard it as mere affectation to use the prefix 'Broughty', the mistake was a natural one and it was nobody's fault that the poor cyclists added eight extra miles to their attempt to cross the Tay.

The Broughty site seems to have been first settled around 6000 BC (see **Stannergate**). Its name was originally Bruchtie, later Brochty (with the same derivation as *broch*—Old Norse *borg*, German *Burg*, all meaning a fort and cognate with English *borough*). The mediaeval settlement of Broughty owes its existence to the fortress which commands the entrance to the inner estuary and which had grown in strategic importance since Dundee Castle had fallen into disuse (see under **Castle**). The castle at Broughty originally stood on a sea-girt rock accessible only at low tide; in the sixteenth century it belonged to Lord **Gray**, who traitorously surrendered it to the English in 1547, thereby allowing them to bombard Dundee with devastating results. The castle fell into ruin and lay derelict for centuries, but was rebuilt in 1860 as a coastal fortification manned by the Forfarshire Artillery Volunteers; thereafter it was used for military purposes until as recently as Hitler's war.

As usually happened, a settlement had grown up around the mediaeval castle, with fishing and ferrying as its main occupations. Broughty Ferry was at one time an important salmon-netting station, replaced later by herring and sprat fishing, and until early in the present (twentieth) century supplied Dundee with most of its white fish. In addition it was for a long time the landfall of one of the several ferry services which operated between the Angus and north Fife coasts, and was known as East Ferry to distinguish it from the nearby landing-stage of West Ferry. The name Broughty at that time referred to the castle, the harbour being variously called Partan Craig ('crab rock') and Port-on-Craig (probably variants of the same name—see **Tayport**).

At the beginning of the nineteenth century a local laird built himself

Broughty House, a grand villa near the castle and immediately to the west of the dock pier; he developed a new settlement ('The New Town at the North Ferry'), and the grid system on which it was laid out is still in evidence in the streets along the shore. In 1826 a regular thrice-daily horse-drawn coach service to and from Dundee was introduced, later to be replaced by the railway. Indeed, it was the opening of the Dundee to Arbroath railway in 1838 which ensured that Broughty Ferry, as it was now called, would really be put on the map. Its elegant station, built at the same time, is reckoned to be the oldest in Scotland and recently achieved the status of a Category A building. It was once the departure point of thousands of Black Watch soldiers in the 1914-18 war, and was until comparatively recently thronged by daily travellers; but now that its great days are gone, the very buildings themselves are under imminent threat of demolition.

With the coming of rail transport, and as the industrial effluent in Dundee grew more troublesome, Broughty Ferry became (in the words of the British Association Handbook for 1912) 'mainly a residential town for wealthy Dundonians' who were 'attracted by the sea air'. The remains of some of their vast palatial mansions can still be seen in the landward part of the village, but the most spectacular of them, Castleroy and Carbet Castle (belonging respectively to the rival jute families of **Gilroy** and **Grimond**) both succumbed to the ravages of dry rot. Broughty Ferry had in fact become a fashionable place (a sort of east coast Helensburgh) and to some extent remains so, vast building developments to the north-east notwithstanding.

But commuter-dom brings its inevitable problems. In 1905 the Dundee, Broughty Ferry and District Tramway began a service of open double-decker cars to and from Dundee (and there are people alive who remember it); but the motor-car has now, with the usual dire results, largely replaced railway and trams (and even buses) as a means of commuter transport. The upgrading of the A92 into a trunk road has bisected the landward part of the former village, and the expansion of the urban transport system transformed Broughty into yet another Dundee suburb.

Fifty years ago Broughty Ferry was still a favourite resort for day outings and longer holidays. A generation hardier than ours used to frequent the beaches there and at West Ferry, and as recently as 1956 a new 'bathing shelter' complete with mod cons such as 'sprays' was provided. Today's Dundonians like every one else have more sophisticated tastes in the matter of vacations—but not too much so. A Dundee wifie, recounting in the baker's her recent Balearic holiday, was asked 'Whaur's Mijorcuh?'; the answer was a snooty 'Eh dinna ken—we *flew*'. Another lady objected strongly when the plane unaccountably took her to 'Mallorca'. But 'The

Ferry' still has its devotees, and on a bright breezy summer's day the sea-front with its castle, harbour and old fisher cottages takes a lot of beating.

Caird

Caird in Scots originally meant a craftsman, later a tinker, and the term was sometimes debased to describe an itinerant pedlar; it is from the Gaelic *ceard*, which can have all of these meanings, and it possibly spills over into the slang term 'card', meaning an oddity.

Edward Caird (1806-1889) was an enterprising young man from Montrose who, in his twenties, started up a textile manufactory which later developed into the Ashton Works in Hawkhill. Caird was one of the first to see jute as the natural successor to flax and hemp; and under the management of his son James the expanded factory became one of the most prosperous in Dundee. Sir James Caird, as he later became, had the reputation of being a forward-looking and benevolent employer with an eye to the welfare of his workers; he was certainly a princely benefactor to his native city, and the name is still a household word in Dundee.

The first memorials that come to mind are the City Square and Caird Hall, which Sir James offered to the city prior to the '14-18 war. The plans in their original form did not entail demolition of the eighteenth-century Town House designed by the celebrated William Adam; it was envisaged that the new hall would be entered through a carriageway on either side of 'The Pillars' (as the old Town House was commonly known). But it was Caird's opinion, not shared by everyone, that the old Town House was no longer sufficiently imposing for a city enjoying an industrial boom; so its preservation was quietly dropped from the planning process.

The design of the entire scheme was to be by the City Architect, James Thompson; but other fingers were stuck into the pie including those of Sir James' half-sister Mrs Marryat who made a gift of money for a rather brutal north-facing colonnade (said to be in recompense for the demolition of The Pillars). When peace-time finally arrived the design concept had further deteriorated; the City Chambers on the west of the proposed square were to be faced by a nondescript commercial development on the east.

The construction works took a considerable time; the old Town House was finally demolished in 1931 amid some bitter protest. Thirty years later the City Square was still being described as 'an aesthetic disaster for which no individual can fairly be blamed'. It is only very recently that some minor but imaginative improvements (including pedestrianisation of the whole area) have transformed the concept into something less forbidding and, on a good day, rather attractive.

Not so controversial were the other Caird benefactions. In 1913 Sir James had bought part of an estate which included Mains Castle policies; he presented them to the Town Council along with funds to create a huge park to include the Den o' Mains, and to lay out golf courses and other recreational facilities. Again the war intervened, but ten years later the Caird Park was opened to the public by Mrs Marryat (Sir James having died in 1916); many a dedicated golfer has taken his first turf on the pleasant sward of the 'Wee Cairdie'. Sir James also provided funding for the acquisition of Camperdown Park, and for additional building at Dundee Royal Infirmary and elsewhere for the purposes of health and welfare.

It would be wrong to omit mention of another Caird dynasty of Dundee, completely unconnected with the jute family. Alexander Caird was a clothier who, with his pony and trap, sold his wares around the hills of the Carse and the eastern glens (unconsciously conforming to the *ceard* of his surname?) and in 1879 he started up as a gents' outfitter in Union Street. Taking his sons into partnership he then founded the firm of Caird and Sons in Reform Street. The firm prospered, and branches were opened in Perth, St Andrews and Elgin; diversification included gents' hairdressing and skiing (possibly influenced by the family's ownership of a house in Glenshee, where they eventually developed their own ski-school). In the 1960s the firm took over the premises of Henderson and Mackay in Whitehall Street for the formation of Cairdsport, with its own dry ski-slope.

Everything looked set for further expansion; but even the best run family firm cannot compete indefinitely with the multiples, and Cairds of the quality clothing alas did not long survive the centenary of its foundation.

Caledon

The Caledon used to be one of the great institutions in Dundee: the sight of the shipyard 'skailing' is something that remains in the memory—the sound of the 'bummers' followed by hundreds of men swarming up to the Ferry Road for their buses, with some on bicycles, but not a motor car to be seen. The experience of seeing a large ship on the stocks, approaching completion, to be followed by a public launch, is something that the young have never enjoyed. The yard is now used for fabrications for the oil industry, but the glamour has gone; and the very name is unsung, unless you count Caledon Street off the Stannergate or the Caledon Jetty beside the eastern wharves—pathetic reminders of a great era.

The shipyard was initially an offshoot of Tay Foundry at Stobswell, a nineteenth-century firm run by W.B. Thomson, which after 1874 concentrated mainly on the building of ships. One of the first big orders was from the earl of Caledon, and Thomson named the shipyard after his client. (The name itself has a certain resonance, since *Caledonia* was what Tacitus called the tribal lands north of the Forth-Clyde line). The yard specialised in the smaller type of steamship, and cornered the local shipbuilding market for most of the nineteenth century. The *Discovery* was built there in 1901. An earlier merger with Robbs of Leith only strengthened the company, which flourished particularly in times of war, when the Admiralty called the shots. The final efflorescence was from 1939 to 1945, and thereafter, despite complete modernisation of the yard and the securing of one or two orders for the largest vessels ever to come out of it, the Caledon gradually went the way of the shipbuilding industry in the west of Scotland. It finally closed its doors in 1983, one of its last major tasks having been the manufacture of box girders for the new Tay road bridge. Given the economic conditions of Dundee in the 1930s it is a miracle—or a triumph of good management—that the Caledon survived for so long.

The success of the Caledon yard was no isolated phenomenon in Dundee. There had been shipbuilding in the old days of wood and sail, and of the five firms building ships in the mid-nineteenth century the most notable was Gourlays; although now largely forgotten it was an innovative and forward-looking concern as well as being in its time a large-scale employer of men. The Gourlay brothers had been in the engineering business since 1790, and were building locomotives for the newly-formed railway companies in the 1830s. They started up in shipbuilding in 1854, having acquired a yard to the east of Camperdown Dock, and between then and the end of the century the firm turned out over 230 steamers. They were pioneers in the use of steel, with steam power and screw propulsion; one of their great achievements was the *Dundee*, commissioned by the Gilroys for the transporting of jute in bulk; another, which demonstrated the firm's flair for elegance and even luxury, was the *London* of 1892.

It is believed that the firm overextended itself financially through a re-equipping of the yard, and it failed finally in 1909. The surname Gourlay has long been a familiar one in Dundee—a Gourlay was hanged for heresy in 1562—and it is a pity that it could not have been preserved in the naming of one of the new streets in Dundee's redesigned dockland.

Camperdown

Kaemperdoen is the name of a village on the north coast of the Netherlands where on 11 October 1797 the British gained a brilliant victory over a Dutch fleet which had recently provoked the London government by insolently sailing up the Thames. The British force was under the command of Adam

Duncan, son of the Provost of Dundee and member of an old Angus family who were sometime lairds of Lundie. The family had a *pied-à-terre* in Dundee, Burnhead House within the cathedral precinct on the castle hill, and known after 1861 as Castlehill House; there Adam was born in 1731. When still a lad he entered the Royal Navy and rose through the ranks to become—fifty years later—an admiral and Commander of the British Fleet in the North Seas. In recognition of his outstanding victory, the Admiral was created Viscount Duncan of Camperdown and Baron Lundie; some ten years later his son Robert became first earl of Camperdown. A grateful nation gifted to the new earl a splendid estate to the north west of Lochee; he commissioned William Burn, a distinguished Edinburgh architect, to build a mansion to grace the parkland; the city being in its usual state of penury, it is believed that Sir James Caird later had to assist in the financing. The result is Camperdown, among the finest mansions in Scotland and now, with the adjacent Templeton Woods, one of the largest and loveliest parklands open for public enjoyment.

The house was completed in 1824, a neo-classical building with a huge pillared portico on the east front with a suite of state-rooms to the south and a magnificent stained glass dome above the hall. Gladstone stayed there for several days in 1869 as guest of the earl, and in the improbable company of Benjamin Jowett. But the house was built for splendour and not comfort or convenience, and it is believed that the later Camperdowns had their modest living quarters in an extension to the north of the house; however that may be, the house became too large and expensive for domestic enjoyment, and the property was acquired by the Corporation of Dundee in 1945. The city authorities were unable to decide what to do with it, and this indecision lasted for some time (although the public were admitted to the grounds in the following year). The mansion itself lay empty for decades; it was for a time the home of the Spalding Golf Museum and was later opened to the public and used as a conference centre with function suite and restaurant; but this arrangement was never entirely satisfactory. It is welcome news indeed that the new Dundee City Council is planning to transform the mansion into a country house gallery. The three main rooms along with the grand hall and staircase will be restored to their Georgian splendour, and, through the good offices of the National Galleries of Scotland, the building will house portraits of the Duncan family and naval pictures relating to the Revolutionary and Napoleonic period; the centrepiece will be the vast picture by J.S.Copley of Admiral Duncan receiving the surrender of the Dutch fleet, which was bought by the Camperdown family and at one time graced the wall of the grand staircase. In addition, some naval memorabilia which have been on long loan to the National Maritime Museum at Greenwich will be returned to the new gallery. A truly fitting use for the building and one that is very much in line with the purposes for which it was originally built.

The Camperdown policies had been adorned by magnificent specimens of hardwood trees, forming avenues and rides, and it was possible for Dundee Corporation to develop part of it as a golf course without harm to the landscape. Other parts of the park have since become a wildlife centre and a children's playground, and by judicious control of traffic and parking the amenities have been successfully preserved. The south-eastern portion of the policies was incorporated into Dundee's new industrial estate, and brought within the city boundary in the immediate post-war years.

If battle there had to be, Kaemperdoen was a good place for it. The name (in its English version) trips readily off the tongue, but if the battle had been at Brouwershaven or Ijmuiden, would either of these names have passed into our vocabulary? As it was, Camperdown entered rapidly into the repertoire of Dundee place-names, and there are at least half a dozen roads, street and places in Lochee, Downfield and Broughty Ferry that make use of it. Most notably, Camperdown works in Lochee, built by the Cox brothers around 1850, was named by them as a compliment to their aristocratic new neighbour. In 1865 a new dock was named after the admiral's grandson, who had made his own way as MP for Forfarshire and was an energetic member of the Harbour Board. For the 1997 bi-centenary of the battle the McManus Galleries mounted a splendid exhibition which attracted more than local attention. In the long term, however, it is Camperdown and its mansion that will provide the most fitting memorial to Dundee's own naval hero.

Castle

Compared with Edinburgh's Castle rock and Calton Hill, the eminences within Dundee's mediaeval precinct are mere molehills. Some of them indeed no longer exist, having been either quarried for their stone or levelled to make way for road developments. Such are Corbie Hill to the north of the Overgate, Bonnethill and Hawkhill. But the most important was the Castle Rock, now occupied by St Paul's Cathedral Church which was built in 1853 and whose situation on a crowded junction site hardly does credit to its fine architecture. This building deserves to be visited more often; and sightseers should note the remaining vestiges of the black dolerite rock on which stood Dundee's earliest fortification.

The early history of the castle is very obscure; that it was in existence in the early thirteenth century is implied by the presence of name 'Castle Wynd' in contemporary documents, but its date of origin is unknown. Tradition says that the castle was surrounded by a large ditch with a drawbridge, and that it figured importantly in the War of Independence, suffering damage at the hands of William Wallace; and it is quite likely, as an anonymous eighteenth century historian reports, that Robert the Bruce in 1314 'had it razed to the foundations that it might no longer Serve the English as that it had done'. The castle must have been of considerable size, since it apparently accommodated 130 knights and horsemen. After the demolition of the castle itself, Castle Hill was used as a sort of moot hill, where justice was dispensed; and there exists an agreement dated 13 August 1384 between the Burgh and the hereditary Constable of Dundee regarding his jurisdiction during the fair, to the effect that 'the Bailies...sall sit upon the Castle Hill with the Constable or his depute' to regulate any disputes.

In the seventeenth century a plan by the Cromwellian governor of the burgh to re-erect the town's defences was initiated but never completed; and it is recorded that the Castle Hill was in the following century occupied by 'a Neat Building Erected by Doctor John Willisen, Physician, in which he dwells, and that large Lodging Lately belonging to Sir George Stewart of Grandtully, in which he long resided' (this latter is possibly the present Castle Hill House, within the cathedral precinct, where the Old Chevalier spent the night of 6 January 1716 during the closing stages of the disastrous Jacobite uprising). Another contemporary writer credits the site with a large statue of Neptune, and an old inn which was formerly the castle's gunpowder store and armoury.

To the east of the rock was the Burnhead, the site of the Castle Mill, which provided a service for grinding grain. The Castle lade, which issued from the dam at Meadowside, provided the water power; the Town Council records for 1521 contain detailed proposals for renovating the mill, including laying 'twa new millstanes of Kyngudy' (i.e. from Kingoodie quarry) and 'redding the Wellgait burn'.

The strongest reminder nowadays of Dundee's castle is the name Castle Street, formerly Castle Wynd. Castle Street in one's youth was a place of great charm, with fine traditional shops at the top and a magical view down to the docks and the vanished Royal Arch. In between was the early nineteenth-century Theatre Royal building, with its bust of Shakespeare (still to be seen at the risk of a cricked neck) and at the foot was the old Coffee House, Merchants' Library and Reading Room; it later became a masonic temple, but was better known to most as David Winters. More recently it was converted for occupation by a restaurant, a pub and a travel agent, but it is still fit to grace what is one of Dundee's nicer thoroughfares.

Claverhouse

One of the most resonant names in Scottish history comes from a small estate three miles to the north of the centre of Dundee, on what is now the city's northern perimeter. Although the name Claverhouse appeared on the Ordnance Survey map, there was little to be seen of it in stone and lime. Claverhouse cottages, near Old Mains church, form an eighteenth-century village street, which may be on the site of the original estate, but the creation of the new Claverhouse Road alongside the old has obliterated all that remained of a village atmosphere; nearby Myreton of Claverhouse and Barns of Claverhouse are farms on the original Graham property, and the Claverhouse bleachfield on the Dighty Water (scene of the dyeing and proofing of the **Baxter** linen products) is still there, the old mill buildings having undergone conversion to become the centre-piece of an extensive—but quiet and attractive—new housing complex. In our unromantic times, however, the name Claverhouse denotes a vast Industrial Estate which covers most of the old territory.

The etymology is obscure, and the name itself would probably have been forgotten were it not for the spectacular career of the Jacobite general, John Graham of Claverhouse, known to his Highland fans as *Iain Dubh nan Cath* ('Dark John of the Battles') and to his Lowland enemies as 'Bluidy Clavers'. This is not the place to recount the man's exploits, first as oppressor of the Covenanters, later as champion of the exiled James II and VII, and finally as the architect and brilliant leader of the first Jacobite uprising. Appointed by the King as his lieutenant in Scotland, he was elevated to the viscountcy of Dundee in 1688, and it was by this title that he was to figure in the history books—not to mention song and story (see **Dundee**). In the same year he became by royal appointment Provost of the city, an office to which however he failed to give his undivided attention; indeed he was continually at loggerheads with the town council of the day.

Claverhouse was born in Angus in 1648, and some twelve years later he and his younger brother were admitted as 'burgesses and brethren of the city of Dundee', in recognition of their family status rather than their achievements to date. The Graham family had acquired the estate of Claverhouse in the sixteenth century, and this remained the family title for many generations until it died with John Graham at Killiecrankie. By 1620 the family had also acquired the castle of **Claypotts**, and twenty years later bought the lands and barony of Glen Ogilvie, south of Glamis. When not absent on military or royal service, Claverhouse spent most of his life in 'the tower, fortalice and manor place of Glen', not a trace of which now remains. It was here that he spent his childhood before enrolling as a student at St

35

Andrews University, and it was at Glen Ogilvie that he took leave of his young wife before embarking on his last fateful campaign. In 1684 Claverhouse had also purchased the estate of Dudhope, which carried with it the hereditary office of Constable of Dundee even although its lands at that time lay outside the burgh boundary.

The city can lay claim to Claverhouse as one of its most inspiring if erratic sons. While his army was composed largely of Highland clansmen, with only a small retinue of Angus men, it was on Dundee Law that on 16 April 1689 John Graham, 'mounted on his charger, brilliant in scarlet', unfurled the royal banner for the war that he hoped would restore his Stewart master to the throne of Britain. A little more than three months later Claverhouse met his death at Killiecrankie from a stray bullet fired at the moment of victory. He was forty-one. Despite the city's anti-Tory politics, then and now, would a cairn on the summit of the Law be an extravagant monument to this remarkable man?

Claypotts

This is just about the most prosaic and unprepossessing name that could have been given to a castle. It must in origin have referred to some long-forgotten clay-pottery in the vicinity, which eventually gave its name also to a main road, and has more recently been adopted by a Terrace, a Place, a Court and Gardens. To imagine the castle in its heyday we must mentally eliminate all these features, including the horrific roundabout; instead, imagine the castle standing on the verge of an ornamental lake (later a skating pond, now drained), with views south over the fields sloping down to the river and north to the Grampian foothills.

The lands of Claypotts belonged to the barony of Dundee and as such came into the possession of David, earl of Huntingdon, at the end of the twelfth century, as a gift from his brother William the Lion. Alexander II granted the feudal superiority of the lands to the Abbey of Lindores, and in the sixteenth century the feu came to be held by John Strachan of the family of Carmyllie. His son, also John, started building the castle in 1569; the initials 'I.S.' ('Iohannes Strachan') on one of the stones with the date 1588 show that the castle took almost twenty years in the building.

Most Dundonians, even those speeding along Arbroath Road, will be familiar with the castle's external appearance, unchanged for centuries. In architectural terms it is a good example of a Z-plan keep, with two circular towers capped with square attic towers, corbelled from below and with crow-step gabling. It is roofed with grey flake stones, as characteristic of Angus as red pantiles are of Fife. A description of the internal layout would be superfluous, for the building is now in the care of the department of Ancient Monuments, and is open to the public. As befits a castle built for security and not for comfort, it is unfurnished; but those who remember it as a storehouse for the adjoining farm (now demolished) will be in for a pleasant surprise: go and see for yourself.

Claypotts Castle has not had a happy history. During its tenure by the Strachans there were attacks, sieges, an attempted kidnapping and numerous matrimonial disputes, often ending in violence. Since ours is an unromantic and incredulous age, we perhaps no longer have need of legends such as that of the white lady who, every 19 March, stands at one of the upper windows wringing her hands and waving a kerchief in the direction of her lover in his castle in distant St Andrews. (The lady is supposed to be Marion Ogilvy, her lover Cardinal Beaton: but the fact that Miss Ogilvy never lived in Claypotts, which in any case is not visible from St Andrews Castle, must render the story apocryphal.)

In the 1600s the superiority of the lands passed to the Scrymgeours, who gave a charter of Claypotts to Sir William Graham of Claverhouse; the property remained in the Graham family for three generations, one of which included John Graham (see **Claverhouse**). This produced a new crop of legends: John Graham, Viscount Dundee, traduced by historians and reviled by the Presbyterian kirk, probably resided from time to time at the castle, but there is no basis for the stories of wild orgies, of witches' covens, bargains with Auld Nick, and other unseemly goings-on which were once associated with Claypotts. Nor do we deal much nowadays with legends of fiery black chargers from the devil's stable nor with the silver button which was responsible for the death of (bullet-proof) Bonnie Dundee; and the baleful fires which were said to light up the castle every Hallowe'en could now scarcely be seen above the lights of Claypotts roundabout.

Clepington

The estate of Clepington lay to the north-east of the Barony of the **Hilltown**, occupying one of the most elevated sites of the town, with an open outlook to the north, east and south. Now that high-rise building has made a nonsense of Dundee's topography, we no longer talk about 'the heights of Clepington', but that is how the place used to be described 150 years ago.

The map of 1821 shows the estate to be completely unbuilt upon, and it was not until later in the century that the area became industrialised. In 1874 Frank Stewart Sandeman founded the Manhattan Works on a 24-acre site in Dundonald Street. Sandeman was an expert in jute preparation and manufacture, and a shrewd businessman, and Manhattan Works were among the best organised in the city. The firm geared its output to the requirements of New York State, and Sandemans' products became much sought-after in the USA. The family name is commemorated by Sandeman Street which runs parallel to Clepington Road.

The area near to the mills was developed in the later nineteenth century to provide affordable housing for the employees and their families. Even today Clepington Road is characterised by the typical Dundee tenement, architect-designed and built of grey stone, erected mainly as a form of speculative investment by middle-class entrepreneurs. Similar tenements are to be found in other areas of Dundee, especially in Hilltown and Lochee; they were built to last, and most of them (after a degree of modernisation) have survived as pleasant and reasonably comfortable dwellings. In appearance they compare favourably with recent corporation housing schemes, and are certainly more occupant-friendly than the 'multis'. Stone tenements ceased to be built by 1914, when they were no longer a profitable investment.

The original estate had been divided into East and West Clepington, each with its mansion and connected by the present Clepington Road, which a century ago functioned as a sort of ring road (not unlike the present Kingsway); in 1912 it was chosen as the site of an experimental trolley-bus route, designed to circle the city and to link Lochee with Broughty Ferry—but the internal combustion engine was to provide an easier option.

The Clepington estate was bisected by the old Glamis Road, which runs north from Dens Road, the southern portion of it having been renamed Provost Road in the present century in memory of a former holder of that office who was one of the Thom lairds of Clepington. The name was also preserved in Clepington School.

The name Clepington means 'Clephan's homestead'; the Clephanes were an ancient and well-known Fife family, whose seat was Carslogie House near Cupar, and who held the barony through twenty generations from the twelfth century; the original Clephan who owned and gave his name to the Dundee lands was apparently of this family, but nobody seems able to identify him. The ending of the name Clepington indicates that it belongs to the period when Scots had replaced Gaelic, for *toun* was the Scots form of the English *-ton* ending—as in Kensington, Darlington and dozens of other southern place-names. So at a guess the estate of Clepington must have been named around the fourteenth century. (The older word-formations in Dundee place-nomenclature are discussed in the **Introduction**).

A Dundee lady in the 1920s used to delight southern friends with her pronunciation of the words 'Clepington Road'—which form a familiar Dundee sound-pattern and one which trips pleasingly off the tongue.

Constitution

Dundee society has always been highly politicised, from the Whiggism of the 1740s through the radicalism of the later eighteenth century, followed by the patriotism of the Napoleonic era and the Chartism of the Victorian times to the Labour movement of our own day. This is reflected in some of the street names, such as Nelson Street and Wellington Street, not to speak of the series named after Victorian prime ministers—Peel Street, North Street, Canning Street, Russell Place and Derby Street (locally pronounced 'Derrby' not 'Dahby'). The most notably political names result from the upheavals of the 1830s and are to be found in the two main north-south thoroughfares of Constitution Road and **Reform** Street.

Constitution Road leads from Bell Street to the upper slopes of the Law, a fact which is no longer obvious now that it has been bisected by the inner ring road. Being one of the steepest thoroughfares in Dundee, it tended to lose its traffic to the other streets which are its offshoots, such as Barrack Road. For the same reason Constitution Road is not residential in character, but has been the location of several public buildings; the most obvious and recent of these are the Dundee College of Further Education and the Infirmary extension, but an earlier one was the Watt Institution, named in honour of James Watt the engineer. The Institution was built in 1838 on a site further down the road, later occupied by the YMCA. The Institute had been founded for 'the instruction of young tradesmen in the useful branches of arts and sciences' (the human face of the Industrial Revolution, if you like) and had earlier functioned from the Hammerman's Hall in Barrack Street. The Institution unfortunately ran into financial difficulties, and lasted for little more than a decade before a combination of overspending and underfunding forced it to close. It was a worthy enterprise which deserved to succeed but whose very existence is now almost totally forgotten. The educational traditions of this area are however being reinforced by the massive new buildings of the University of Abertay.

The naming of Constitution Road embodied a word seldom found in the Dundee household vocabulary and one whose associations are probably no longer remembered. It has posed minor problems for officialdom. The story used to be told of a horse toiling up Constitution Brae (as it was familiarly called) and succumbing to the weight of the cart and the steepness of the gradient; a constable was summoned to the happening (a familiar one to older Dundonians) and when his diligence was found to exceed his literacy in recording the locus of the accident he was heard to exclaim 'Ach, drag the beast roon the corner tae Bell Street'.

Cox

This surname is not Scottish in origin, although familiar enough in this country. The Dundee Coxes originated in a family called Cock that are thought to have come here from Holland in the sixteenth century, possibly on account of religious persecution there; they changed their surname to Cox at the beginning of the nineteenth century. James Cock or Cox set up as a linen manufacturer at Lochee-field in the early 1700s, using the cloth supplied by the local handloom weavers and the water supplied by the Lochee burn (now invisible but remembered in the name of Burnside Street). His descendants continued the business in a steadily successful way; by 1793 the family owned 280 handlooms. After a fire in 1816 which destroyed the warehouses they bought some property at Foggyley and built a new mill and weaving sheds. The succession of James Cox to the headship of the firm in the 1820s was a turning point, and when in 1841 James assumed as partners his three brothers William, Thomas and George, the enterprise really took off. The expanding firm rapidly outgrew Foggyley, and in 1850 Cox Brothers bought a large site at nearby Harefield which they promptly renamed as a compliment to their new neighbour the earl of Camperdown. The secret of their success was that Cox Brothers were the first firm to concentrate on jute, power-looms having been introduced five years earlier; it has been said that what the Baxters were in flax and linen the Coxs were in jute.

The aim of Cox Brothers was self-sufficiency, and Camperdown Works was conceived on a huge scale (200 acres eventually, the largest jute factory in the United Kingdom), with its own branch railway, stables, foundry, 'half-time' school and fire station, and in its heyday giving employment to more than 5,000 workers. Cox Brothers still had to rely on the import of raw materials from abroad, but they took steps to change that in 1862 when they established their own jute presses near Calcutta. William Cox even became seized with the idea of owning and operating an independent carrier fleet, and in 1874 joined with other entrepreneurs to found the Dundee Clipper Line. One of the ships was called the *Maulesden*, after William's stately residence near Forfar; normally used for transporting jute from India to Dundee, she diversified in 1883 by carrying 500 emigrants to Australia.

Not much remains of the Cox empire in the collective consciousness of modern Dundee. A little-known memorial stone in Dargie kirkyard in Invergowrie outlines the Cox history, mentioning the various family seats of Foggyley, Clement Park and Beechwood; an old table-tombstone in Liff Parish kirk records the death of James Cock and his wife Isobel Doig in 1742. But there is not much else: Cox Street in Downfield is hardly a fitting memorial to this once mighty Dundee family, and in any event probably commemorates James Cox in his capacity as Lord Provost (1872-75).

The firm name was lost in 1920 when it joined the Jute Industries consortium, although occupying the former Cox office at the east end of Bell Street and having Ernest Cox as first chairman. The family's extensive properties in and around Dundee were dispersed: Clement Park became a maternity home early in the present century, and **Beechwood** was demolished to accommodate a slum clearance project some time later. Foggyley reverted for a time to being a Cox residence, but now houses families who are very possibly descended from former Cox employees.

The Camperdown Works site has been almost completely cleared of factory buildings, which have been replaced by a complex of shops, cinemas and restaurants. All that remains is the Silver Mill, which has been converted to housing. The outstanding feature of the Works was a gigantic campanile or bell-tower, standing over 280 feet tall, with elaborate and Italianate decoration; built at the height of the firm's prosperity in 1865, it represented the triumph of a jute dynasty, but was (with typical dismissiveness) known to generations of Dundonians as Cox's Chimney Stack. This is practically the only visible survivor of the original Works, and it has given its name to the whole complex—Stack Park (but how many people make the mental connection?). For a memorial to the Coxes perhaps we shall have to make do with the campanile, a landmark visible from places as far apart as the summit of Ben Lawers and the pier at St Andrews.

Craigie

The Gaelic word *creag* (a rock or crag) occurs many times as a place-name on the map of Scotland; around Dundee there are several examples including Craigowl, Craigton, Craigend, Craigwell, Lang Craig, Scotscraig and Bottomcraig. And in the Highlands there are literally dozens of hills called *Creag Dubh* ('black rock'). Craigie comes from the adjectival form *creagach* meaning 'rocky', and it is not surprising that it should have been the name of a large estate on the outskirts of Dundee—the name of Craigie Quarry is indicative of the nature of some of the terrain.

The size of the original estate is indicated by the surviving district and street-names which incorporate the word Craigie: although the mid-point of the estate was probably round about where the Eastern Cemetery now is, we also have the names of Mid Craigie and Old Craigie Road, with Craigie Street (off Albert Street) on the west and Craigie Drive on the east. The **Morgan** Academy was built on part of the Craigie estate. Milton of Craigie refers to 'the mill farm of the estate', and Strips of Craigie to an early form of cultivation, but names such as Craigielea and Craigiebarns are probably just modern inventions. Craigiebank, perhaps the most familiar form of the name, appears in the street directory only under the entry 'Craigiebank Terrace', which forms part of Pitkerro Road; but most Dundonians would nowadays associate Craigiebank with the garden suburb designed in 1919 'for workers', consisting of steel houses with pebble-dash rendering built on a concentric plan, with Greendykes Road as its main artery and with the later addition of Craigiebank Church at its hub. If only all of Dundee's suburban planning had been as inspired as this.

In the Middle Ages the lands of Craigie belonged to Isabell de Brus, daughter of David, earl of Huntingdon, and wife of Robert de Brus, ancestor of King Robert I. Around 1240 she granted the lands to the abbey of Lindores near Newburgh in Fife, founded by her father. Craigie remained the feudal property of the abbey until the mid-sixteenth century, and was tenanted successively by the Scrymgeours and the Wedderburns. By the 1770s the property appears on the old maps as being in two halves, with Craigie proper on the east and Wallace Craigie (so-called because of its proximity to the Wallace burn—see under **Wallace**) on the west.

Wallace Craigie was acquired in 1779 by George Constable, a friend of Sir Walter Scott. It is reputed to be the original of Monkbarns in *The Antiquary*, and a charming description of the eighteenth century mansion is given in the novel. Mr Oldbuck (the antiquary of the title) is discovered by his new friend sitting under an old holly tree 'with spectacles on his nose and pouch on side, busily employed in perusing the *London Chronicle*, soothed by the summer breeze through the rustling leaves, and the distant dash of waves as they rippled upon the sand'. The mansion of Wallace Craigie must have been on the east side of the present Dens Street, not far from the shore, and it takes a bit of imagination to conjure up today the idyllic scene described by Scott.

Constable's heir in entail was Lawrence Brown-Constable. The estate was broken up in 1828 and sold off as building lots to the north of the present Ferry Road, but the survival of these two surnames in Constable Street (a continuation of the Cowgate) and Brown Constable Street (leading north to Dura Street) are there to remind us of the existence and location of the estate of Wallace Craigie. The southern portion had earlier been feued to a family called Black (hence Blackscroft) and changed hands several times in the next 200 years; it remained as 'a piece of corn-land' until it was first built upon some time after 1730. Before the construction of the Camperdown and Victoria docks and the reclamation of the land on which Dock Street was built, the gardens of the houses sloped right down to the river. The transformation of the scene was completed in 1836 with the construction of the Wallace Craigie Works, built by William Halley, and still operational.

Crichton

The first Dundee infirmary opened in King Street in 1798, the precursor of the later **DRI**; one of its most gifted surgeons was Dr John Crichton, a native of the city and son of a Dundee bailie. Born in 1772, he studied medicine at Edinburgh University, settled in Dundee as a young doctor and remained there for the rest of his long life. He seldom left Dundee, and is reputed to have been so content with his home territory that he never ventured furth of Scotland. His specialty was lithotomy (removal of bladder-stones) and he carried out this pioneering operation more than two hundred times. Most of his patients (whose ages ranged from two to eighty-five) made a successful recovery, only fourteen deaths being recorded.

This eminent and well-loved local surgeon however had his awkward side. He owned a large house on the south side of the High Street, an area which then consisted of narrow wynds negotiable only by pack-horses; the present Couttie's Wynd gives some idea of what it must have been like. In 1779 the Town Council decided to create a new thoroughfare to connect the High Street with the harbour, which at that time consisted only of the area later occupied by Earl Grey Dock. It was not long before the 'New Street' itself proved too narrow to accommodate the increasing volume of horse-drawn traffic, and when road-widening plans were prepared it was found that the house of Dr Crichton stood directly in the way. There were prolonged and acrimonious negotiations between the doctor and the Council, and not until it was agreed to name the new street after him would Crichton consent to sell.

Crichton Street was the first post-mediaeval street in Dundee and as such was an important thoroughfare. The older (west) side is a pleasant array mostly of traditional shops, including a pub called 'The Pillars'; this used to be the popular nickname of the old Town House, a scale model of which is to be seen above the pub's entrance. The east side is completely occupied by the not very attractive backside of the City Chambers and the Marryat Hall. The former charm of Crichton Street has largely vanished, for it now peters out amid the confusion caused by Tayside House and the convolutions of the road-bridge landfall; and its importance has been diminished with the downgrading of the once-busy Shore Terrace to the status of a car park.

No doubt Dr Crichton would have sounded the 'ch' in his name as in 'loch', but for generations the street-name has been pronounced like 'criton'; indeed the alternative spelling Crighton has elsewhere become more common. The name comes from a combination of the Gaelic word *crioch* ('end') and the Scots *toun*—with some such meaning as 'boundary village', as in Crichton in Midlothian.

The good doctor survived until 1860, by which time the street had become an established part of Dundee's shopping and commercial centre; but one must doubt if he would have been pleased by the present-day appearance of the street for which he had reluctantly sacrificed his residence.

Dalgleish

The surname Dalgleish comes from the Gaelic *dal glas* which simply means 'green field'. There were apparently lands of the name in Selkirkshire; and indeed the Border family of Dalgleish in the sixteenth century had the reputation of being a wild and lawless people.

Not so Sir William Ogilvy Dalgleish, Bart. Born in 1832, he was a respected Dundee citizen, a prominent member of the firm of **Baxter** Brothers & Co Ltd, and a generous benefactor to the city of his birth. His final gifts to his fellow-citizens, shortly before his death in 1913, were stained glass windows and an electric lighting system for the Albert Hall (see **Albert**); the benefaction was completed by his son the following year.

In 1860 in the early years of his marriage he resided at Mayfield House in Arbroath Road (then on the outskirts of the town). On his death the house was sold at a reduced price to provide a hostel for the students of Dundee Training College; with many alterations and extensions the property continues to be a student residence. When a street was constructed near Mayfield to connect Arbroath Road with Broughty Ferry Road, it was named Dalgleish Road in memory of this benevolent baronet whose life, beginning in the year of the great Reform Bill and ending just before the First World War, covers the whole of the Victorian and Edwardian eras, with a year or two to spare at either end.

Dalgleish cannot be called a common surname, although it is justly celebrated in soccer circles; there are no more than twenty occurrences of it in the current Dundee telephone directory. But most of Dundee's residents and commuters to the east will be familiar with Dalgleish Road even though they do not concern themselves with the story behind the name.

Dempster

Dempster is a fairly common surname in Dundee; it is really 'deem-ster', someone who deems or judges (the old phrase 'for doom' at the end of a judicial sentence means 'for judgement'). In practice the dempster was the officer who pronounced judgement on behalf of the court, and the office tended to become hereditary: Andrew Dempster who lived in Menmuir around 1350 was dempster to the Abbot of Arbroath.

In 1677 there was born in Monifieth a George Dempster whose family was to play a modest but notable part in Scotland's agricultural and political history. Dempster settled in Dundee as a young man and acquired a house in Rankine's Court on the north side of the High Street. No humble dwelling this, however, for courts such as these often contained the townhouses of the gentry, and Dempster's dwelling was described as a mansion.

Unbeloved by the inhabitants of Dundee, who suspected him of profiteering as an exporter of grain, Dempster had to face a mob who raided his house in 1720 during a time of famine. Nevertheless, George Dempster and his son John continued to prosper as merchants and bankers, and acquired successively the Angus estates of Newbigging, Laws, Ethiebeaton and Dunnichen. It is with the last-named of these that the Dempster name is now associated.

George Dempster of Dunnichen, born in 1732 and grandson of the original George, was educated at the Grammar School in Dundee, then at St Andrews University where he won the coveted medal for archery. He became an advocate in Edinburgh, practised at the bar for a time, and was an accepted member of society in the Edinburgh of the Enlightenment; but having inherited a large fortune from his father he relinquished the legal profession and turned to politics.

In the days before the 1832 Reform Act, Dundee had to share its Member of Parliament with other burghs, including Forfar, Cupar and St Andrews. In 1762 George Dempster was elected member for the Forfar and Fife Burghs, a seat which he held for 28 years, despite his extreme radical views: in 1790 he sent the congratulations of the Whig Club to the President of the French National Assembly on 'the triumph of liberty and reason over despotism, ignorance and superstition', a gesture which can hardly have endeared him to the patriotic British establishment. But shortly thereafter he decided upon another career-change and absorbed himself in agriculture and fisheries; it is as an agricultural improver and author of *A General View of the Agriculture of the County of Angus* that he is now best remembered.

His declining years were spent between Dunnichen and St Andrews, a pattern of living not untypical of Dundonians who have made their pile. He was for a time Provost of St Andrews, and Dempster Terrace in that town is named in his memory (which is more than happened in Dundee).

'Honest George Dempster' is reputed to have been the exception to

Walpole's rule that every man has his price; and William Pitt recognised that there were still people like Dempster who could not be bought. Dempster died in 1818 in his 87th year, respected by all and loved by most (although his puritan disapproval of the theatre irritated a few of his contemporaries). His many achievements included the financing of the construction of the Inchcape lighthouse and the foundation of the Dundee Banking Company in 1765, which made available the necessary capital for the expansion of the flax industry in the town. He was a worthy man, deserving of at least some recognition in his native city.

Dens

Den was an Anglo-Saxon word meaning a valley; in England it very often appears as *dene*, and in Lowland Scotland it almost always refers to a steepsided glen (the Den of Mains provides a convenient example). Such was the area in Dundee known as 'the Dens', described in lyrical terms two centuries ago as 'a deep and narrow glen, whose grassy banks used to be redolent with wild flowers and shaded by great trees'. With the culverting of streams and the levelling of knolls, nearly all traces of the original den have long since been effaced; nevertheless, when driving up or down Dens Road, it is still possible to imagine oneself in the contours of the eighteenth century landscape.

The Dens burn rose somewhere to the north of the Law, ran approximately along the line of the present Dens Road, under the Victoria Bridge (at the junction of Victoria Road and Arbroath Road) and down Dens Brae. An alternative name for it at one time was apparently the Butter (really 'bitter') burn, which survives in several street names and in that of a school. To begin with, the stream and its tributaries were used in a modest way to provide for the needs of the cottage industries of weaving and spinning. The harnessing of water power however was the key to the large industrial developments of the early nineteenth century, and Dens will always be associated with the activities of Baxter Brothers, whose industrial head-quarters were the Lower Dens Works in Princes Street. (The **Baxter** family is so important in Dundee as to deserve an entry to itself). The Upper Dens mills were equally busy, and in their heyday in the 1850s the two were together employing more than 5,000 workers—although of course by this time the mills were powered by steam, and a location close to running water was no longer necessary.

The little Dens burn had by this time outlived its usefulness as far as industry was concerned, and was being described as '...no other than a torrent, which tended to dry up in summer'; culverting was to be its fate.

The Dens mills concentrated initially on flax and linen and only later turned to jute, but they eventually joined in the general collapse of the industry and closed in 1978; a few years later the wheel had turned full circle, and the impressive buildings of the Upper Mill (designed by the Baxter's own engineering partner, Peter Carmichael) have now become dwelling-houses in an imaginative and award-winning conversion.

Dens is an important name in Dundee, Dens Road being one of the principal thoroughfares from Victoria Road to the northern part of the city. Even better known outside Dundee is Dens Park, the home of the Dark Blues or Dundee Football Club.

Dighty

The Dighty Water rises in the Sidlaws above Lundie, flows in a wide sweep round the north of Dundee and enters the Tay estuary at **Monifieth**. Its older spelling was 'Dichty', which gives the correct pronunciation but is not of much help with the etymology, which remains obscure; and the valley which it drains was formerly known as Strath Dichty (a term which still figures in the hereditary title of the earls of Strathmore and Kinghorn). With the boundary extension in 1939 the Dighty was brought within Dundee's city limits, and subsequent housing developments have created several trans-Dighty suburbs such as Whitfield and Fintry.

The valley of the Dighty was originally part of the old earldom of Angus. It is not known whether the Angus earls had a residence in 'Strath Dichty' although tradition credits them with a castle near the site of the existing Mains Castle. There is a reference in 1551 to 'the Mains of Erlis Strathdichty', which is to be interpreted as the home farm of the earls, and it is likely that the more recent parish name is an abbreviation of this. (Mains Castle would therefore be named after the parish, which was later to be linked with its neighbour under the title 'Parish of Mains and Strathmartine' —see separately under **Mains** and **Strathmartine**).

The Dighty may tend to be undervalued and unrecognised by the people of Dundee and Angus, but this was not always so. In the seventeenth century map it is correctly given the status of a river, flowing through a strath, and by all accounts it was a watercourse of great natural beauty. But once the water resources of Dundee had been exhausted (see **Dens**) the town's manufacturers turned their attention to the streams of the hinterland. There had been corn mills on the Dighty from time immemorial, but in the eighteenth century manufacturing industries began to make their appearance in the form of 'waulkers', who scoured their woollen cloths in the upper reaches of the burn (waulking or fulling is the process of thickening cloth by means

47

of soaking, beating and shrinking). Next came the harnessing of the Dighty waters to form a series of mills and bleachfields in connection with the burgeoning linen trade; this was an initiative of the town authorities in the 1730s, who controlled a string of dams between Strathmartine and Panmure; all of these are now derelict although some are still to be seen (see **Claverhouse**). It is reckoned that by the beginning of the nineteenth century there were over sixty mills powered by the waters of the Dighty.

Dereliction led to neglect, and even the name of the stream came to be disregarded: in its upper reaches it has appeared on the map as 'the Dronley burn' (it flows past the hamlet of that name) and at its mouth it acquired the name of 'the Milton burn' (from a farm and a mill at Monifieth). The poor old Dighty has suffered the fate of many another bonny Scottish stream: integrated with urban industrial development and despoiled for its water-power in the eighteenth and nineteenth centuries, it has largely been written off in the present century. But this need not be so: paradoxically, the Dighty is now less polluted than at any time in the last three hundred years. The upper reaches were always clean, but between Strathmartine and Monifieth it was the chemicals used for washing and bleaching linen that caused the pollution. Due to the strenuous efforts of voluntary groups, vast amounts of rubbish have been removed from the bed of the stream; the result is that nowadays the water looks as clear as a Highland burn and you can see herons fishing in the old millponds—indeed a nearby private housing development has earned the name 'Heron Rise'. At Trottick the waterside has been given Grade A status by Dundee Council in its Nature Conservancy Strategy, and commended for its 'rich and varied wildlife'.

A guide book of a hundred years ago described Bridgefoot in these terms: 'there is a quiet sylvan beauty about the scenery here that might tempt you to linger and lounge on the parapet of the old bridge'; later visitors have found it easier to resist any such temptation: there are indeed stretches of the river that are still a litter-infested eyesore, and progress is always liable to be nullified by vandalism. But the situation is not irremediable: the Dighty could be made as attractive as the Water of Leith now is, and a twelve-mile walkway from its source at Lundie to its mouth at Monifeith would be an asset to the new generation of ramblers. This might also bring the name Dighty properly into the Dundee vocabulary in a way that is more meaningful than the random adoption of the names Dighty Place and Dighty Gardens for streets in Menzieshill.

Docks

Dundee is not, like Southampton or Sydney, a natural seaport: the Tay estuary can be a wild place, and the unpredictable action of the river never permitted much in the way of natural anchorages. Dundee's harbour probably started with Scouringburn Creek (see **Scouring Burn**), where boats would be dragged up the mud flats for security; later the little bay between the Castle rock (see **Castle**) and St Nicholas Craig (later the site of Craig Pier, near Discovery Quay) would give a measure of protection from the current.

Although the existence of a shipping harbour that was more than merely a natural haven is implied in William the Lion's charter to the burgesses of Dundee, the first mention of an actual structure is in 1255, when Alexander II granted a licence to the Abbot of Coupar Angus to export wool and other merchandise to Flanders. A further charter in 1458 ordered the enlargement of the harbour, and a hundred years later a levy of four pence was imposed on each vessel arriving at the port, in order to pay for the upkeep of the harbour.

After the middle of the sixteenth century more extensive works of excavation and construction were put in hand, although the harbour remained essentially a tidal basin liable in turn to scouring and silting. The harbour was almost destroyed in 1600 by a great storm; and as if natural disasters were not bad enough, the sacking of the town by General Monck in 1651 completed the destruction of the port. The fact that the General seized sixty vessels before destroying the port is an indication of the size it had then attained; and we know from other sources that the city was already a prosperous mercantile centre with extensive trading links with the Continent (see **Baltic**).

In the 1720s Daniel Defoe reported disparagingly that 'Dundee had but an indifferent harbour'; he described it as being more in the nature of a basin. Later in the century the harbour consisted of little more than the Craig Pier on the west side, a breakwater on the east side and two piers at right angles to the breakwater, with the harbour mouth in between. It is only in the nineteenth century that we are able to speak of a dock rather than a harbour in Dundee, and even then the innate conservatism not to say obstructionism of the town authorities had to be overcome before real progress could be made (see **Riddoch**). The year 1815 saw the transfer of ownership of the docks from the town to a Commission which was to carry out improvements suggested by the consultant engineer, Thomas Telford. Extensive new works were put in hand, including the opening of a graving (or dry) dock, and, a decade later, the King William IV Dock. An Act of 1830 vested the docks in the harbour Trustees; there followed extensions to the east, including the Earl Grey Dock (an enclosed harbour with cast-iron lockgates, and named after the reforming prime minister); and in 1848 the east tidal harbour was formed, later to become the Victoria Dock and the Camperdown Dock. At the end of the nineteenth century, with the textile boom at its height, a contemporary writes of the jute-laden vessels from India which 'form a yearly argosy far exceeding in value and importance those of Ragusa and Venice'.

In *Treasure Island*, Jim Hawkins' visit to Bristol takes him, to his delight, 'along the quays and beside the great multitude of ships of all sizes and rigs and nations'. Judging by the late-eighteenth century drawings, Dundee was just like that. But in modern times the new class of large vessels found the docks inadequate, and the continued silting of the Tay was problematical. By the end of the nineteenth century every ship calling at Dundee had to be lightened before it could enter the dock. The King George V Wharf was built in the deep water in 1913/15; and most of the large shipping is nowadays to be seen along the wharves which stretch east to the Stannergate. Of the original seaport, all that remains are the Camperdown Dock and the Victoria Dock, with the frigate *Unicorn* tucked into the southwest corner. The naval presence (a submarine anchorage) was removed from the King William IV Dock after the '14-'18 war; and the Earl Grey Dock was filled in to create the road bridge landfall in the 1960s.

Dundee's dockland was constructed entirely on ground reclaimed from the river, and this includes Dock Street itself. It is hard nowadays to believe that Yeaman Shore ran along the beach, and that between Craig Pier and Stannergate was a large bay, now totally reclaimed and built over—not once but several times. To the west of Craig Pier was another wide bay—discussed under **Riverside**. While the annual tonnage of shipping using Dundee docks is probably greater than it ever was, the city has lost the tang of the sea and the sense of being a port.

Also gone is the domestic bustle that must, a century ago, have been seen at the docks. There were steamers to London on Wednesdays and Saturdays from the Camperdown and Victoria docks; to Hull once a week, every Wednesday; to Newcastle once a week, and to Liverpool every Tuesday. Pleasure trips to Newburgh and Perth operated daily during the summer months. How pleasant it all sounds to jet-age ears.

Draffen

It used to be maintained that Dundee was a city without a middle-class; on the one side were the landed county families and industrial magnates, and on the other a large undifferentiated urban proletariat. While this is a gross over-simplification, it is true that between the wars the class which embraced the professions and small businesses was very coherent and identifiable: in other words, everybody knew everybody else. This particular sector of society could almost have been characterised by one word—Draffens.

The firm started in a small way in the Overgate in 1833 (at that time reckoned to be the best shopping street in town) when George Draffen, a draper from Coatbridge, saw the possibilities of expanding his business in Dundee. Draffens were pioneers in the method of fixed-price selling instead of the usual process of bargaining. The Overgate 'shoppie' was soon abandoned in favour of a purpose-built store at the top of Union Street; and when Whitehall Street was constructed in 1886 the firm moved to newly-built premises (those currently occupied by Debenhams), considered at the time to be the last word in luxurious shop architecture. The business was at this time (1889) run by George Draffen and his brother-in-law John Jarvie, and the firm traded under the name of Draffen & Jarvie until the latter was bought out in 1891; the grander name of 'Draffen of Dundee' is still to be seen on the brass plate in Whitehall Street. From then until the retiral in 1962 of George, great-grandson of the founder, Draffens was a family firm with a very closely-controlled share capital. Members of the family, who were intimately involved in the day-to-day running of the business, became well-known characters in the eyes of their clientele: the story is told of a garrulous customer asking Miss Draffen if her brother was excited about his forthcoming visit to South Africa, and the reply—'my brother never gets excited but is viewing the event with pleasurable anticipation'.

After George Draffen's retiral there was some further expansion of the firm, when it acquired the Whitehall printing works of William Kidd; but for administrative reasons all the family shares had been sold to the parent company (Blyths Ltd of Edinburgh) and it was only a matter of time before the business was acquired by one of the multiples—in this case Debenhams.

It was the rival firm of D.M. Brown who had conceived the idea of adding a tea-shop for the comfort and convenience of customers; Draffens followed suit, like drapers in many other cities, and it was the restaurant which gave the Dundee emporium its particular ambience. Although luncheon and tea were available, it was at morning coffee time that Draffens became the hub of Dundee society, where bridge-hands were mentally replayed and where reputations were made and unmade. It is not surprising that such coffee-rooms should have attained tremendous popularity in the days before most wives were gainfully employed and when the centre of town was only a ten-minute, twopenny tram-ride away from home. The distinction of Draffens was that virtually the same crowd went there every day, and a newcomer was subjected to discriminating appraisal from the habitués.

In theory, Draffens' drapery departments were open to everybody but, as with the Ritz hotel, you needed a certain confidence to enter the portals. By the end of the Second World War however the process of democratisation had advanced so far that some not-so-genteel mothers were shopping at Draffens; on one recorded occasion a scandalised shop-assistant had to accede to the request of a mother to 'lat the wean treh the coat oan' when the cleanliness of the child was far from being apparent. But times changed, and exclusiveness was something that Draffens could no longer afford, although their high standards were maintained to the end of the era of the large family business.

Draffen as a surname comes from the lands of Draffan in Lanarkshire (there is also a farm called Draffin near Coupar Angus); it is uncommon but was at one time extremely well-known in Dundee. Nowadays there are no bearers of the name in the city, and the only two Draffen telephone subscribers are at the time of writing to be found in Fife.

DRI

'*Inn* is the name of a traveller's home / *Fir* is the name of a tree / *Mary*'s the name of a girl, and / There's only one in Dundee'. Why do these childish jingles remain in the memory, when much more important things are forgotten? This particular riddle is worth recalling only because, in the fairly near future, there won't *be*, for the first time in two centuries, a Royal Infirmary in Dundee.

The story begins in 1798 when the first infirmary opened on a site between King Street and Victoria Road. Built by voluntary subscription, it took over and was combined with a former dispensary, catering mainly for out-patients but providing forty beds. A charter granted by George III in 1819 gave it the title 'Dundee Royal Infirmary and Dispensary'; six years later the number of beds was increased to 110. But the town's growing population, and the frequent incidence of epidemic disease, made new arrangements necessary and in 1852 the foundation stone of the present DRI was laid by the Duke of Atholl. (The old infirmary became a lodging house, and was demolished to make way for Victoria School, itself cleared for the housing development at Ladywell Avenue).

The site of the new DRI was to be an open terrace to the east of Dudhope Park and alongside the old Dundee-Newtyle railway line; the British Association handbook of 1912 describes it as a 'a site which, for openness and healthiness, would be difficult to equal in any city'. The architects (a London firm) were chosen as a result of public competition, and the winning entry was a vast and pretentious neo-Elizabethan pile of suitable grandeur for a city enjoying a commercial boom, but hardly tailor-made for a functional hospital by today's standards. The money was again raised by public subscription, but the initial capital of £14,000 soon proved inadequate to provide the facilities required. Later in the century additional buildings were provided by private benefaction: they included nurses' accommodation (funded by **Gilroy** and **Dalgleish**) a maternity unit (by the Forfarshire Medical Association) a maternity nurses' home and a cancer pavilion (both by **Caird**). In 1898, with the opening of the Medical School, DRI attained the status of a teaching hospital.

Thus developed the DRI, which for the best part of a century fulfilled the medical and surgical requirements of Dundee's population, and for which generations of citizens have cause to be grateful. To begin with, it was thought in some quarters that the provision was over-generous and that Dundee had acquired a white elephant (the same was said about Ninewells— strange how history repeats itself). But this prophecy was shortly to be dispelled, and plans to transfer the whole unit to Ninewells were being considered soon after the completion of that complex (see **Ninewells**); work on the Ninewells extension is now at an advanced stage.

What will become of the old DRI? Although completely taken for granted by Dundonians, it is still a notable Victorian building, with its central gatehouse flanked by great towers; but the trouble is that the public has no access to what was meant to be the impressive main entrance, and the mass of the building is dwarfed by high-rise flats to the north and surrounded by a clutter of unimposing annexes. Traffic and parking problems are becoming unmanageable: it is inconceivable that a hospital building on the lines of 'the DRI' would be erected nowadays: in short, if you wish to look at the history of the last 150 years, compare DRI with Ninewells. And yet you will still find many who have a soft spot for the older establishment, with its homey familiarity and intimacy and—yes—its essential Dundee-ness.

Dudhope

Who the Dudda was who gave his name to the little 'hope' (or valley) on the northern outskirts of mediaeval Dundee is something that we shall never know (not that it matters much). Even so the lands of Dudhope can be identified long before the fifteenth century, when the **Scrymgeours**, Hereditary Constables of Dundee, started building a fortress there, the family's earlier residence in the Castle of Dundee having been destroyed in 1314 (see under **Castle**). More than twelve generations of Scrymgeour held office as Constable, which was a high-ranking state office (the title is from the Latin *comes stabuli*—'count of the stable'); there was a short interregnum in 1683-4 during which the office was held by the Earl of Lauderdale; the Dudhope property then passed to the powerful Graham family, through the marriage of Matilda, daughter of Sir James Scrymgeour of Dudhope with John Graham. From this union came the Grahams of **Claverhouse** (a family so important to Dundee that the name deserves an entry to itself). After the death of Claverhouse and the extinction of the viscountcy, a grateful King William gifted Dudhope Castle to the Douglas family. The post of Constable lapsed with the abolition of heritable jurisdictions following the failure of the '45 Rising, although the title remained with the Douglas family until as late as 1877.

Dudhope Castle, although a fine baronial mansion in a strategic situation above the town, cannot claim to have seen much of the action. An instrument of torture known as The Maiden was housed in the castle, no doubt as part of the Constable's judicial equipment, but no details remain of its use. The lands and castle were sequestrated by the Regent Arran in 1547, by reason of the current Constable having traitorously signed the capitulation of the town to the besieging English army. King James VI was entertained at Dudhope in 1617 on his way to Skye; John Graham of Claverhouse did not live long enough to enoy its amenities to the full or to test its strength.

By the eighteenth century Dudhope Castle was becoming derelict; an observer of the 1770s reports '…the Palace is now running fast into decay, as they are keeping no more of it in repair but the South side of the Fabrick, which is the dwelling of the Factors of the Lordship'. Matters did not improve when it was leased for use as a woollen mill; but the threat posed by Revolutionary France resulted in it being re-roofed and converted into a barracks in 1799. A separate barrack block (now demolished) was added to the east of the castle, and for the next century the whole property was known as 'the Barracks'—hence Barrack Street, the lower part of the road leading to the castle from the High Street. It was from these buildings that the Fourth Battalion Black Watch left on 23 February 1915 for France and the battle of Loos, which precious few survived. The now decrepit castle became a storehouse and an eyesore to generations of Dundonians. It is however a mark of Dundee's new awareness of its heritage that this attractive white-washed building, on a terrace overlooking the Tay, has been restored by the City to some of its earlier glory and is now occupied by the Dundee Business School attached to the University of Abertay.

The castle gardens, known as 'The Pleasance', were crossed by a public pathway, more or less on the line of the present Lochee Road. Access to the west was by several country lanes or 'loans'; the word was corrupted to become Loons Road. On the haugh below the castle there was a mill, probably near or on the site of the later Dudhope Works in Douglas Street and powered by the **Scourin Burn**.

Towards the end of the eighteenth century the rest of the Dudhope estate began to be divided. The northern part was bought by a Perth merchant named Rankine (whence Rankine Street), and one of his descendants sold the bit comprising the Law and its southern approaches to the Town Council in 1878 for the sum of £3,888. At about the same time, other parts of the property were sold as a prestigious building development, giving us streets such as Dudhope Terrace, Prospect Place and Albany Terrace

Dundee

The first thing to be said abut the name Dundee is that it cannot be a reduction of the Latin phrase *Dei donum*—'gift of God'. These two words do not even sound like the name of the town (which in its earliest recorded spelling was Dunde): *Donum Dei* would be inferior Latin but might make more sense. No, we have to regard *Dei Donum* (words which appear on the city's seal in 1416) as a piece of late mediaeval punning, devised by some Latinist as a compliment to the place, and possibly intended to recall the earlier legend of the town having been founded as a thank-offering by David, earl of Huntingdon (see under **St Mary's**). A modern parallel would be Professor Douglas Young's clever tongue-in-cheek suggestion of a motto for his home town of Tayport—*Te oportet alti ferre*: the Latin words sound much the same as 'Tayport ferry' but the meaning ('you ought to be borne to the heights') is of course entirely different.

The Renaisssance humanist George Buchanan also gave a latinised version of the city name, to wit *Taodunum*, which seems to presuppose an etymology involving the name of the river—possibly 'fort on the Tay'. There is however no documentary evidence that this form of the name was ever current, and was certainly not in vernacular usage.

The plain truth appears to be that the name comes from *dun Deagh*, the first component being the Gaelic word for a hill or fort and the second from a Celtic personal name *Daigh*, which possibly meant fire. The reference is thought to be to the Dundee Law, which is known to have been fortified from about the fourth century, and still is the most prominent landmark in the area.

It used to be said that, like *Dei Donum*, the term 'Bonny Dundee' was appropriated by the city for propaganda purposes, and that the description 'Bonny Dundee' was meant to apply to John Graham of Claverhouse, Viscount Dundee—a man whose handsome good looks could not be denied even by his enemies and which were recorded for posterity by Sir Godfrey Kneller, the fashionable portrait-painter of the day. But it is now recognised that Sir Walter Scott, when he wrote the words of the celebrated song about 'the bonnets o' Bonny Dundee', took his inspiration from an earlier Scots ballad whose refrain was 'I daurna stay longer in Bonny Dundee'— a clear reference to the town.

It may be the case that the modern city no longer deserved the appellation 'bonny', and in the 1930s there was in circulation a comic postcard showing the view from the Law of a filthy and smoky industrial landscape with the sardonic caption 'Bonny Dundee'. It is true that mills and factories were to Dundee what churches and palazzi are to Venice; although we have progressed beyond that now, it is to be feared that by the time the city regains its pre-industrial beauty the term 'bonny' may have disappeared from the vocabulary.

Oddly enough, Dundee never became a surname in Scotland (as did Glasgow, Aberdeen and Stirling). The name of the eponymous hero of the cult movie *Crocodile Dundee* must have been an invention of the film-makers.

The pronunciation of the the name of our city has never caused problems. One used to be able to recognize Glaswegians from their habit of pronouncing the name Din-*dee*, with the stress heavily on the second bit, but nowadays this is not so often heard. Natives balance the stress equally on both syllables like a see-saw; so, fortunately, do incomers.

Dunsinane

In the triangle formed by Coupar Angus Road, the Kingsway and King's Cross Road there is a collection of street-names called after places in the Sidlaws—Dronley Avenue, Kilspindie Road and Hatton Place to name but a few. The best-known is Dunsinane Avenue, for it gave its name to an important industrial estate which now dominates this part of the city.

How ought this name to be pronounced? It is derived from the Gaelic *dun*, meaning a hill or hill-fort, followed probably by *sinean*, meaning breasts (or just possibly from a personal name); in either case the hill-name would be pronounced 'dun-sinnen'. Shakespeare seems to follow this pronunciation in a rhyming couplet in *Macbeth*, when the three witches prophesy that 'Macbeth shall never vanquished be until / Great Birnam wood to high Dunsinane hill / Shall come against him'. But the metre in other references seems to demand a stress on the final syllable: 'Till Birnam wood remove to Dunsi*nane* / I cannot taint with fear'; and the matter is more or less clinched in the most famous couplet of all 'I will not be afraid of death or bane / Till Birnam Forest come to Duns*inane'*. The average Dundonian quite properly pronounces words without reference either to Shakespeare or to Gaelic etymology; but one would imagine that the name is more commonly (if less correctly) stressed on the final syllable.

Dunsinane is one of the most attractive hills in the Sidlaw range, between Collace and Kinnaird, and its summit bears on the map the legend 'Macbeth's Castle'. Popular tradition has it that Macbeth met his end in battle here, and a large flat stone slab called the 'Lang Man's Grave' used to be pointed out as his resting place. But one must remember that practically no facts about the historical Macbeth are known for sure, and it is equally likely that it was at Lumphanan in Aberdeenshire that he was killed. It is not even certain that he murdered Duncan, usurped the throne or embarked on a life of bloodshed. Shakespeare was not writing history, and anyway took the plot of his play from a *Chronicle of Scotland* written by an Englishman called Holinshed; but so much is true, that Dunsinane is only twelve miles from Birnam (well within half a day's march), that the summit was at one time fortified, and that the terrain fits well with the denouement of the play. Birnam Hill is still wooded, and visible from Dunsinane; but Macbeth's sentries must have had very keen eyesight to have known where the mobile forest came from. (For those who have forgotten the plot, an army led by Malcolm and Macduff, passing by the wood of Birnam, hack down the leafy branches to camouflage themselves, thus setting at naught the comforting prophecy of the witches).

But enough of literary exegesis. Dunsinane has a beautiful sound to it, however it is pronounced, and justifies its place in Dundee's repertoire of Sidlaw names, along with Craigowl Road, Kinpurney Place, Carlunie Road, Denoon Terrace, Hayston Terrace and Kincaldrum Place. It might be added that we also have a Birnam Place, definitely not visible from Dunsinane Drive!

Dura

Dura Street runs between Dens Road and Albert Street, and was in the heart of Dundee's factory-land. The street clearly takes its name from the Dura works, which were built there by the firm of J & W Walker about 1836. But how Dura works acquired its name is a more interesting story.

The clue is surely to be found in the proximity of Dura Street to Kemback Street, which runs north from Arbroath Road. As every Fifer knows, Dura Den is a beauty spot in the parish of Kemback near Cupar; and it happens to have been the location of Blebo mills, a flax spinning concern on the River Eden run by one John Walker who was born there in 1812. His son Harry was one of the pioneers of the spinning of jute yarn and founder of the firm of Harry Walker & Sons of Dundee. It is possible that the webs of linen woven in these Fife villages were sent by the Walkers to Dundee for processing, or that bales of finished cloth were sent there for warehousing and eventual sale when the market was at its most favourable. Eventually the Walkers transferred their business from Dura Den to Dundee, no doubt because of the emergence of jute in preference to flax as the raw material for spinning and weaving.

The manufacture of linen, one of Dundee's staple industries from the mid-eighteenth century to the mid-nineteenth century, started with small rural manufactories in villages in the city's hinterland. One such was at Glamis (see under **Baxter**). Others were purpose-built settlements for hand-loom weavers, like the village of Dairsie which was founded in 1800 on one of Fife's main roads; it was at first named Osnaburgh, osnaburg being a coarse type of linen which was originally made in Osnabruck in Germany. (Dairsie was the parish name; Osnaburgh still appears on the Ordnance Survey map as an alternative name, and although it has not been used for many years, it was recently revived as a street name in the village.)

Several of the early linen works had been converted corn mills, and the waters of the River Eden in Fife and its tributary, the Ceres burn, had proved particularly suitable for flax processing. The villages of Dura and Kemback were among the riverside settlements associated with spinning-mills. These mills represented little more than a cottage-industry, and were often operated by farmers as a part-time occupation; but they must eventually have achieved sufficient importance to give their names to two streets in Dundee's industrial heartland.

Dura works survived the lean years of 1837, 1847 and 1857 and were carried on by a Walker descendant. The original firm of Harry Walker & Sons opened extensive new factories in the Clepington lands, including Caldrum works in St Salvador's Street. Caldrum works in its day had more spindles operating than any other in Dundee with the exception of Camperdown works (see **Cox**). A grandson of the original John Walker of Dura Den founded the firm of P.G. Walker & Son, owners of Balgay works in Lower Pleasance (see **Balgay**). The family, despite its extensive business interests in Dundee, wisely continued like many another to reside in the pleasant valleys of North Fife.

Dura as a place-name is from a Celtic word *dubron* meaning water, found in various forms all over the British Isles from Dover to Aberdour. Kemback was originally Kenebach and is probably from the Gaelic *cinn beag*—'at the little headland'. These provide examples of pleasant-sounding

Dundee street-names, taken from agreeable places, but used to describe the location of the darkest of Satanic mills.

Fintry

This well-known Dundee name was adopted in order to identify a council housing scheme built in the 1950s to the east of the Forfar Road on the northern outskirts of the city.

Fintry embodies the Pictish words *fionn* (white) and *tref* (place, stead), and the street names in the scheme were studiously taken from other place-names containing the syllable *fin*. Thus, Finavon Street, Findhorn Street, Findowrie Street, Finella Place, Finlow Terace: truly a celebration of white-ness—and the name of the adjacent Whitfield has of course the same sense.

But all this is somewhat fortuitous, for the name Fintry was brought to these parts by the family of Graham who held the lands of Fintry in Stir-lingshire. The Grahams—not a Highland clan but a Lowland family—accompanied the earl of Huntingdon (brother of William the Lion) to Scot-land on his return from England in 1124; the family rose to great prominence in the wars of Wallace and Bruce but were unjustly deprived of the earldom of Strathearn in the early fifteenth century. A branch of the family had acquired lands in Angus which earned their owners the earldom and later dukedom of Montrose; hardly less notable were the Stirlingshire Grahams, one of whom, Sir Robert Graham of Fintry and Strathcarron, married a Scrymgeour of **Dudhope**. From this union came the junior branch who took the designation of **Claverhouse** from their newly acquired estate of that name; the other branch retained their title of Fintry, and gave it to the castle which they commenced building in the Den o' Mains (see **Mains**).

The Grahams had always been a royalist family and were to continue so for at least another two centuries. Sir David Graham, builder of Mains cas-tle (or Fintry castle as he would have called it) had supported the Roman Catholic church during the reign of Mary Queen of Scots; he was impli-cated in a plot, known to history as the Spanish Blanks, and when it failed he became the scapegoat, although several high-ranking nobles (possibly even the king, James VI) were mainly responsible. He was executed in 1593.

Thereafter the Grahams of Fintry fade into relative obscurity, leaving the honours to their kinsmen Montrose and Claverhouse. They retained their lands however until the early 1800s, and the last of them, Robert Graham (a friend of Robert Burns—see under **Linlathen**) was forced for financial reasons to sell the lands of Fintry to David Erskine, an Edinburgh W.S.; and although Graham retained the territorial designation 'of Fintry' he moved with his family to the nearby estate of Duntrune. The Grahams went to the Cape during the South African wars; and the settlement of Grahamstown was named after the thirteenth laird of Fintry, 'in testimony of the services of Colonel Graham, through whose exertions the Caffre hordes have been driven from that valuable district'; thus the family name and fame were to be preserved on another continent.

The remains of the Graham family vault can still be seen in the old Mains churchyard just across the den from the castle. But as a Victorian guide book delicately puts it: 'The kirkyard…was enclosed some years ago to exclude the rough idlers from Dundee, who turned the sacred spot into a gambling and drinking saloon on summer Sundays'. If only the writer could see it now, with never a tombstone at the vertical. Among the (designedly) horizontal slabs is one which covers the remains of Clementina Stirling Graham of Duntrune, a sprightly Georgian lady of Sir Walter Scott's acquaintance whose pleasant habit it was to mystify house guests by impersonating an ancient country spae-wife and to tell them home truths which they had much rather not have heard. Her little book, called simply *Mystifications*, is still worth reading.

Fleming

Think of the Fleming Gymnasium, one of the early buildings of Dundee University College (as it then was); think of Fleming Gardens, off Provost Road, originally a slum clearance but now a douce wee residential area; think of Ian Fleming, creator of James Bond, and of his less celebrated but more appealing brother, the explorer and author Peter Fleming: what do all these names have in common? Answer—a very remarkable Dundee family.

It is no accident that Fleming is a familiar and respected surname in Dundee; the word means a Flemish person, someone from Flanders. The Flemings came to Scotland in large numbers in the mediaeval period; the attraction was the wool trade. Frequent cargoes of Scottish wool and sheepskins left Dundee harbour bound for Bruges in Flanders as well as for other ports in the Baltic; and Flemish traders began to form little colonies in various parts of Scotland, including the upper Clyde valley and Dundee.

Moving on a few centuries, a descendant of one of these traders, Robert Fleming by name, was born in Liff Road in 1845, the son of a factory foreman. Like many another bright Dundee youngster, he won a bursary to the **High School** and became a confidential clerk with **Baxter** Brothers, in the export department. This was at the beginning of Dundee's greatest prosperity: there was growing demand for linen and jute products, engineering in Dundee was flourishing and there were no fewer than five shipyards active in the town. At least half of Dundee's textile products were sent to America, where coarse linen was required as wearing apparel for Negro slaves, tarpaulin for covered wagons, sails for American ships, sacks for cotton and barley and many other uses. With the outbreak of the American Civil War in 1871 this export business took off in a big way as demand grew for military material in the form of sandbags, tents and gun-covers. So it came about that, with plenty of spare capital for foreign investment, the eyes of Dundee's businessmen turned westwards.

Chief among the manufacturers were the Baxters, a large proportion of whose output was destined for the USA in the form of linen fabrics. (Baxters were to linen what the Coxs were to jute). In 1870 Robert Fleming had been sent by Baxters on the first of his many visits across the Atlantic (there were to be more than 128 in all) and he immediately realised the investment potential of this vast half-empty continent. In 1873 he formed the first of five trusts which were to inaugurate a decade of prodigious overseas investment and to make the fortunes of some of his fellow-Dundonians.

Fleming's investments were mainly in railroad bonds, and the issue of shares in the First Scottish American Trust was over-subscribed; its success was followed by the formation of other trusts, and Fleming became immensely rich. By now in his early forties (and having married a young Dundee girl) he migrated to London to become a merchant banker. Fleming was not of course the only investment manager in Dundee: the most famous trusts of all were the Alliance and Second Alliance, founded and run by William Mackenzie, and in their time the largest investment trusts in Europe. Nor was all investment in railways; there were huge speculations in real estate in America, the game being to purchase vacant land and retain it until the selling price was right.

Of course the bubble had to burst: by the mid-1880s the guiding hand of Robert Fleming was no longer present in Dundee, there was a recession in the jute industry and the railroad companies had run into engineering and legal difficulties. Of the land speculations only the Matador Land and Cattle Company was ultimately successful, Fleming having arranged a buy-out of the American owners by his Dundee investors.

There were those who rightly deplored the tremendous outflow of capital from a city with more than its fair share of social deprivation. It was reckoned that, at its height, the amount of Dundee's investment abroad was the equivalent of two billion pounds in today's money: why, it was asked, wasn't some of it used to improve Dundee's industrial infrastructure and to provide decent housing for the urban poor? A fair question, but probably little would have changed. A recession in jute was inevitable when India entered the field, heavy industry was in decline, and nothing could have protected Dundee from the slumps that were to occur with depressing regularity.

As it was, a handful of Dundonians made vast fortunes. The widows of shrewd middle-class investors who had bought a few Alliance or Scottish American Trust shares were able to live comfortably in Downfield or Wormit for the remainder of their days. To the poor, investment was something they might (but probably couldn't) read about in the *Courier*. Inward investment might have given Dundee some civic building, although one Caird hall is quite enough; and the city wasn't quite ready for the type of large civic university that had begun to appear in England from the 1860s onwards.

Whatever the rights and wrongs, the Fleming story shows that it was possible for a Dundee family in three generations to progress in status from factory workers to merchant bankers and fashionable authors of international celebrity. This may have been common enough at the time but seldom happens now. Robert Fleming's is the archetypal success story, and if his local benefactions do not amount to more than Gardens and a Gymnasium, there is still his grandson Ian's literary creation—the ever-popular 007, a dubious literary monument to which Dundee has laid no claim.

Geddes

Sir Patrick Geddes, although not a Dundonian either by birth or residence, was one of the group of brilliant professors who were appointed to the new University College in Perth Road in the 1880s; the others included (under their later titles) Sir William Peterson, Sir Alfred Ewing, Sir D'Arcy Thompson and Sir William McCormick—a galaxy of talent not usually found in a provincial university. Geddes is commemorated in the name of a quadrangle which is part of the Physics precinct—probably the architectural showpiece of the whole campus.

Geddes was brought up in Perth, then resident for a long time in Edinburgh; and although his tenure of a professorship of Botany in Dundee lasted for over thirty years his appearances (like those of his botanical specimens) were in the summer term only. Indeed, his appointment to the Dundee chair was something of a fix, to compensate him for failure to secure a similar appointment in Edinburgh. (But no discredit to Geddes, for that is how things were done in those days—a family doctor could become almost overnight a professor of Anatomy and a parish minister might publish learned monographs on Old Testament Theology.)

It was in the very different spheres of sociology and town planning that

Patrick Geddes was to make his mark: his ideas had considerable influence locally, and provided the inspiration for the plans of James Thomson (City Architect from 1904 to 1924) for the reconstruction of Dundee. So although Geddes was only an honorary citizen of Dundee, whose fame was made in the wider world, his name is a convenient pretext for a word about the early history of university education in the city.

Although the foundation of University College was due to the generosity of the **Baxter** family, the inspiration was of a wider social and intellectual nature, similar to that which had led to the creation of colleges in many industrial cities in England. The original members of staff were mainly young incomers, and were appalled by the contrast between the affluence of the mill-owners and the poverty of the workers. The Dundee Social Union and the Grey Lodge settlements were two of the results of this awakening social conscience in the city. The staff and students of the nascent UCD had an influence on the outlook of Dundonians which was out of all proportion to their small numbers.

The College (founded in 1882) originally operated from two Victorian villas in Perth Road, then a quiet and pleasant thoroughfare; its outlook over the green Fife hills was charming, but behind were the slums of Hawkhill and the industrial squalor of the Scourin Burn mills. This odd state of affairs persisted for more than 80 years. There was a young Oxford mathematician appointed to his first lecturing post in UCD in the early 1960s (spot the anachronism—UCD had become Queen's College in 1953). There were still only the beginnings of a campus, and access to the college from the north was through insalubrious streets and lanes. The Oxonian used to describe his amazement at the sight of distinguished profs picking their way through knots of Dundee urchins brawling or playing 'bools' and 'peevers' on the pavements, and he likened the whole scenario to that of a Charlie Chaplin film.

As early as 1909 there had been plans for the building of a complete college with interlocking quadrangles on the Cambridge pattern. But these never materialised (probably because of lack of funds), and the Geddes Quadrangle is only a vestige of what might have been; the name is also a reminder of the College Garden which Geddes laid out, with 'order beds' showing the evolutionary classification of plants as well as ornamenting the campus—all unfortunately gone.

During its 14-year period as a component of the University of St Andrews a somewhat unstructured building programme was implemented in Queen's College, Dundee (although the Arts Tower Building and Library of 1961 were highly successful). After the foundation of the University of Dundee in 1967 a range of treasury-funded buildings replaced the hovels of Hawkhill; the result is an impressive modern university—but the magic is still to be found in the original parts of the quiet old College above the lawns on Perth Road.

Gilroy

The name of Gilroy is that of one of the major jute dynasties in Dundee, second only to **Baxter** and **Cox**. If it is fading in Dundee memories, it was very vivid to our great-grandparents; and the vast facade of the former Tay Works in West Marketgait indicates the importance of the Gilroys at the height of their success. It is a bit late to view the palatial splendour of the Gilroy family residence in Broughty Ferry, for it succumbed to dry rot and was finally demolished after the last war. The Gilroy story is not untypical of Dundee—lowly beginnings, rising to great power and influence, eventual decline—but still leaving an indelible mark on the city's history.

The three Gilroy brothers, Robert, Alexander and George, began in a small way as spinners of flax and tow in the east end of the town, later moving to a hand-loom factory at Rosebank. In 1848, when jute was coming into its own as the textile fabric of the future, the Gilroys made the necessary change and acquired new premises which they quickly extended. The manufacture of jute goods brought rapid financial success, and in 1863 the brothers built the first stage of the Tay Works in Lochee Road (as it then was). Completed in 1865, the Works was among the largest textile mills in the United Kingdom; it still dominates the northern part of West Marketgait.

With their accustomed business acumen, the Gilroys saw the importance of controlling the supply of their raw materials, and acquired lands near Calcutta for the cultivation of jute; they also ventured into the shipowning business for the purpose of importing the crop. What the Gilroys and others like them could not have foreseen was that the Indians would develop their own industrial expertise and eventually put the Dundee mills out of business. For the time being Dundee remained the jute capital of the world, but by the last quarter of the century the days of rapid expansion and vast profits in the jute trade were nearly over, although few thought so at the time. In 1877 the one surviving brother, George, took his two sons into partnership, and the firm successfully continued for another fifty years as a limited liability company. But the end of the Great War saw the virtual disappearance of overseas markets, and it was not long before the whole jute industry was forced to diversify: the insertion of the word 'Carpet' into the title of Tay Works is indicative of this process. The formation of Jute

64

Industries Limited in 1920 represented a rationalisation of the industry, and several of the city's major firms—including Gilroy Sons & Co—were incorporated into it.

Personal prosperity had enabled George Gilroy to build the private family residence of Castleroy (1867), on what were then the rural outskirts of Broughty Ferry. In mock-Tudor style, it was an enormous and lavishly decorated conception, a statement in stone of the family's pre-eminence in jute. Only the Jacobean gatehouse in Hill Street survives to remind us of Castleroy's past splendours. But the last of the Gilroy sons died in 1923, and although plans were laid for Castleroy to become the property of the community, the dry rot beat them to it. Tay Works was too solidly built for demolition in the 1960s, and instead underwent sensitive conversion to shops and housing. Its richly ornamented facade remains as a reminder of the great days of jute and the part that the Gilroys played in its manufacture.

The members of the family, unlike their rivals the Baxters and the Coxes, did not make their mark in national politics or local affairs; nor were they public benefactors like the Cairds. No Dundee streets, parks or public buildings are named after the Gilroys. Their disappearance from the Dundee consciousness is even more complete than that of the commodity from which they made their fortune.

Glamis

Away from the centre of Dundee, most of the main thoroughfares are named after the neighbouring towns which they serve; examples from east to west are the Arbroath Road, the Forfar Road, the Coupar Angus Road and the Perth Road. This is the situation in most cities, and Dundee is in no way remarkable. The fact that we don't talk about 'the Blairgowrie Road' is no doubt because in pre-industrial times that place was much less significant than the abbey of Coupar; and at the city's eastern end the road to Carnoustie starts off as Broughty Ferry Road, goes into reverse with the title of Dundee Road and then adopts no less than seven different names in its progress between West Ferry and Monifieth, before lapsing into the anonymity of the A930.

An interesting anomaly is Old Glamis Road, which starts from Clepington Road, crosses the Kingsway, traverses Trottick and then leads due north until it is impeded by the *massif* of Craigowl in the Sidlaws. True, a track used to lead over by Gallow Hill, but it cannot ever have been a carriageway. In effect, Old Glamis Road does not lead to Glamis.

It must have been a substantial bridle-path at one time, and it is certainly the most direct route to Glamis as the crow flies. Also it debouches in Glen Ogilvie, a little valley which not one in 10,000 of Dundonians would be able to locate but which was quite important at one time—and famous as the childhood home of Graham of **Claverhouse**. The new Glamis road takes the easier route by Tealinghill and Lumley Den.

If you were to start from, say, Emmock and to proceed down Old Glamis Road in a southerly direction, and to ignore the street-layouts and building developments of the past two centuries, you would find yourself going in an almost straight line down to the Hilltown and the Wellgate. So the no-menclature of Old Glamis Road would be very meaningful to a traveller leaving the City centre. (By way of contrast, the other Glamis Road, lead-ing from Perth Road to Ancrum Road and with its offshoots of Glamis Terrace and Glamis Drive, was named in modern times for reasons of pres-tige; so was Glamis Street in the Hilltown.)

Glamis was a celebrated mediaeval thanage ('Glamis thou art, and Cawdor, and shall be king hereafter' as the weird sisters told Macbeth). Its castle is the seat of the earls of Strathmore; and it was sufficiently prestig-ious to give its name at a recent date to two other streets in Ninewells —Glamis Drive and Glamis Terrace. The etymology of the name is some-what obscure: it is probably from the Old English *cleofan* 'to cut', which has its equivalent in the obsolete Gaelic word *glamphus*—so Glamis would mean something like 'cleft', a reasonable enough description of its situa-tion in a gap to the north of the Sidlaws.

Many of the Angus nobility had town houses in Dundee. An example is the earl of **Airlie**, whose property to the south of Hawkhill is remembered only by the street name Airlie Place; the laird of **Strathmartine** had a fine dwelling (on the site of the Nethergate Business Centre) called Strath-martine's Lodging. But no such arrangement seems to have applied to the Strathmore lords of Glamis, despite the family's extensive Dundee con-nections: Strathmore Avenue does not refer to the earldom, but is part of a naming exercise of the early twentieth century (see **Introduction**).

Gowrie

As every schoolboy knows (or used to be supposed to know) Kenneth mac Alpin achieved a union of the kingdoms of the Scots and the Picts in or around the year AD 843. This was largely at the expense of the Picts, whose territories had for long been undergoing penetration by Vikings as well as Scots; but the union as far as we know was a peaceful one and produced the nation that became modern Scotland. The Scots had invaded from Ireland around AD 500 and set up a kingdom called Dalriada, roughly co-exten-sive with Argyll; four of the sons of the royal house of Dalriada, named respectively Angus, Loarn, Comgall and Gabran, were granted tracts of land in Argyll, and when the Scots expanded eastward some of the old Pictish territorial divisions were re-named after them. **Angus** has been discussed separately, Loarn became Lorn, Comgall became Cowal; and Gabran traditionally gave his name to Gowrie.

The land of Gowrie was originally a mini-kingdom stretching as far as Strathardle in the north, to Kinnoul in the west and to Coupar Angus and Invergowrie in the east. In the Pictish period it had been the territory of the High King, with Scone as its symbolic centre. The Carse of Gowrie refers to the alluvial plain of the Tay, and stretches more than half way to Perth. Blairgowrie meant 'the field of Gowrie', *blar* being one of the many Gaelic words for field, and sometimes meaning 'battlefield'. In Dundee these two names are usually referred to in their shortened forms as 'the Carse' and 'Blair', although 'Blair in Gowrie' had to be distinguished in formal usage from 'Blair in Atholl'.

We no longer think in terms of the Land of Gowrie, and the modern associations of the name are mainly with the village of Invergowrie, which is in fact on the very eastern fringe of what was the old kingdom. Until the eighteenth century however the name Invergowrie usually denoted not so much a village as a parish (which later became Liff and Benvie) and part of a country estate extending as far east as Menzieshill and having Invergowrie House as its epicentre. (The term *inver* means a confluence, and indeed there are two streamlets which converge to the north of the village to form the Invergowrie burn, which watered the bleachfields of Bullion and drove the flour mills and later the paper mill.)

The original settlement of Invergowrie—a mere hamlet, comparable in size with the neighbouring quarry settlement of Kingoodie—was to the south of the present village, and has a long history. It used to be maintained that the old church of Invergowrie (a much more ancient foundation than even the ruined Dargie kirk) was the first Christian edifice north of the Tay; and a somewhat improbable legend credits King Alexander I with having built a palace in the vicinity.

The modern village of Invergowrie dates from 1825 when part of the lands of Mylnefield were feued for building; its rapid development thereafter is largely a result of the routing of the Dundee-Perth railway line along the north shore of the Tay; the establishment of a bleachfield and later a paper-mill at Bullionfield added further impetus. Invergowrie never turned its back on the agricultural hinterland to become a dormitory like Broughty Ferry; but has maintained at least some of its old Perthshire identity despite having developed extensively—and on the whole pleasantly. Invergowrie

House has however become isolated from the village by the new bypass and is now subject to the magnetic attraction of **Ninewells**.

It might well be argued that Gowrie is not in fact a Dundee name, that the Gowrie conspiracy of 1600 was not the city's concern and that the operations of the Gowrie Housing Association almost four centuries later are by no means confined to Dundee. Gowrie is found as a surname in Perthshire although, oddly, not in Dundee. But there is a Gowrie Street off Blackness Avenue, a Gowrie Place off Hawkhill, a Gowrie Court in Charleston and a Gowrie House at Liff; and when we use the word, as we often do, it is pleasant to think that we are commemorating a Pictish kingdom and a Celtic princeling of great antiquity.

Gray

The House of Gray is a splendid mansion lying to the south of Liff village, and across the road from Liff Hospital. Built by the 10th Lord Gray in 1716, from designs by William Adam senior, it underwent years of complete neglect in the present century, from which it is only now recovering. The House of Gray is, along with Gray Street in Lochee and Gray Den near Invergowrie, the only memorial to a local dynasty which was as remarkable in its way as the Grahams or the Scrimgeours. The Grays as a family exhibited over the centuries a very unusual mixture of steadfast loyalty and base treachery; perhaps because of the latter they have not been celebrated in the history of Dundee to the degree which they deserve.

The name of Hugo de Gray is recorded in the district as early as 1248. The family came from England, although it is possible that they were of Norman origin. Sir Andrew Gray joined with Robert the Bruce in the Wars of Independence and was granted lands in the Longforgan district early in the fourteenth century. His descendant, also Andrew, assisted in the liberation of James I of Scotland from the English in 1423, and was held as hostage by them for a further three years. For his services he became Master of Household to the king, and was created a Lord of Parliament as Lord Gray in 1437. Up until that time the family seat had been Foulis Castle near Liff, but Lord Gray proceeded with royal permission to start building another near Longforgan; this was, confusingly, later called Castle Huntly because of the marriage of a subsequent Gray heiress with one of the Gordons of Huntly. Another of Lord Gray's services to his king was to take responsibility for the murder of the earl of Douglas in 1450; for this the Church required him to do penance, which took the form of endowing the church of Foulis Easter as a collegiate chapel, with a provost and a group of prebendaries; the result of the penitent lord's beautification is still to be

68

seen in this remarkable building, which somehow survived the depradations of the Reformers.

Andrew, 2nd Lord Gray, obtained a charter to the 'rock and castle of Bruchty' (see **Broughty**); a man of great ability, he was appointed High Sheriff of Angus, an honour which remained in the family until the reign of Charles I. But he later conspired against James III and was implicated in the king's murder in 1488. Patrick, 4th Lord Gray, connived in allowing the strategic fortress of Broughty to fall into the hands of the English in 1547.

Patrick's son, later 5th Lord Gray, had been taken prisoner at the battle of Solway Moss in 1542 and released on a ransom of £500; although called to meet Mary Queen of Scots on her return from France in 1561, he appears to have veered to the side of the Reformers shortly afterwards.

Patrick, 6th Lord Gray, a curious mixture of treachery and talent, was a figure of truly Satanic dimensions: as Master of Gray, he had been entrusted by Mary Queen of Scots to negotiate her release from prison in England. The Queen was out of touch with her Scottish lords, and not fully aware of the hostility of her son (later James I & VI); she may have had doubts about the Master (she later described him contemptuously as *ce petit broullon*—'this little troublemaker') but she did not know at the time that he was in fact a convert to Protestantism and in league with James. The Queen never recovered from his betrayal of her, which entailed her confinement in England until her execution in 1587.

The subsequent Lords Gray were more loyal to their sovereigns, and indeed lost heavily by taking the royalist side in the Civil War; Andrew, 7th Lord Gray, fought in Montrose's army in 1646 and went into exile with Charles II in 1663; to add insult to injury, the Cromwellian General Monk occupied Castle Huntly. The 8th Lord had to part with large portions of his estate to meet the exactions imposed on his family; all that they retained was the right of burial within the church of Foulis Easter. But the Gray dynasty was by no means finished: John, 9th Lord Gray, obtained from James II a gift of £1,500 (a vast sum in the 1670s) in recompense for the losses that the Grays had sustained for their attachment to the House of Stewart. It is the only recorded instance of such repayment ever having been made. It may have been as a result of this windfall that John, 10th Lord Gray, built the House of Gray referred to in the first paragraph. Not only that, but he landscaped the environs of Liff much as they are today, and pioneered some major agricultural improvements including the growing of potatoes. It is perhaps ironic that it was through his marriage to the daughter of the laird of Kinfauns that the Grays removed from the Dundee area; Francis, 14th Lord Gray, built the castle of Kinfauns, and thereafter the Lords of Gray largely relinquished their Dundee connection. Not completely, for there were at one time branches of this landed family at Invergowrie, Bandirran, Pittendrum, Baledgarno, Balgillo and Creechie; indeed thay seem to have had something of a monopoly of landownership in the locality.

But although most of the Grays may have departed, it is heartening to be able to record that at long last the House of Gray is undergoing restoration, as a hotel and conference centre, with a golf course in the policies. Visitors from the city may again become aware of the legacy of the Gray family and its importance in the history of Dundee and indeed of Scotland.

Grimond

The name Grimond to most people will recall Lord Jo Grimond, one-time leader of the Parliamentary Liberal Party and MP for Orkney and Shetland from 1950 to 1983. Jo Grimond had no apparent connection with Dundee, having been born in St Andrews and educated at Oxford. Yet this charming and modest man was the descendant of a family of Dundee textile tycoons whose power was enormous and whose life-style was conspicuous in its wealth and its extravagance.

The story starts familiarly enough. The Grimond family originated in Blairgowrie where they started up in a small way as a flax spinners; Joseph Grimond, born in 1821, came to Dundee as apprentice to a flax merchant and after a period in Manchester set up in 1847 the business in Dundee of J. & A.D. Grimond first in Maxwelltown (see **Introduction**) and a decade later in the newly-built Bowbridge Works in Dens Road. The works were sumptuous in external appearance, with a magnificent gateway surmounted by a camel (the symbolism is no longer obvious, but was not meant to be associated with the last straw). They were also noted for 'their perfect equipment with the newest machinery and the best appliances'. Not only that, but the needs of the workers were met by the provision of a 'comfortable dining-room, lavatories, and a large hall for amusements'.

Once the workplace of 3,000 people, the works were pulled down in 1987—in the words of an industrial archaeologist 'Dundee's biggest architectural loss since the demolition of its William Adam town house in 1930'. But the firm's former office is still to be seen in the rather odd bow-fronted Georgian building in the angle formed by the junction of King Street with the Cowgate. This was also the family home at one time, before urban squalor began to drive out the mill-owners to the fashionable suburbs. Joseph Grimond chose Kerbat House in Camphill Road, Broughty Ferry, an existing villa which probably took its name from the Kerbet Water in Angus; he renamed it Carbet Castle, and over the years added various extensions of a more and more flamboyant nature. The belief locally (and it was no doubt true) was that Grimond was activated by a sense of rivalry with the nearby Castleroy (see **Gilroy**). Although not so large as Castleroy, the fittings and decoration of Carbet Castle were even more lavish and included a painted ceiling by Charles Frechou, designer of the Palais Garnier in Paris (the ceiling was fortunately dismantled and saved for posterity). But dry rot attacked Carbet Castle, partial demolition was carried out between the wars, and all that now remain are a photographic record of the house with its extraordinarily opulent fittings, and the baronial gate-lodge in Camphill Road.

J. & A. D. Grimond diversified into the jute carpet trade and established the Maxwelltown Carpet Factory, where the first Dundee carpets were woven. When the jute industry was rationalised immediately after the First World War, Grimonds became absorbed into Jute Industries Limited. There is only one Grimond in the current Dundee phone book (although numerous Grimmonds); where have they all gone to? *Où sont les neiges d'antan?*

Harris

In 1819 William Harris, a baker by trade, was enrolled as a burgess of Dundee; an incomer (but from where?—Harris is an English surname), he joined with his brother in a family bakery business which operated in an entry off the Nethergate, soon to be known as 'Harris's Close'. William had a son, born in 1806; young William attended the local Grammar School, but the early death of his father put an end to formal education, and in his teens he entered the family bakery as an apprentice. His journeyman years were spent in London, and he returned to Dundee in 1831 to set up business for himself, in premises at 3 Nethergate; the enterprise was carried on there until quite recently, by Nicoll & Smibert Ltd.

In addition to his bakery concerns Harris diversified into milling and dealing in corn; he immersed himself for a time in municipal affairs, joining the Town Council in 1842 and being appointed a bailie in 1847. Having grown very rich and successful, he devoted his later life to philanthropic concerns, particularly those of an educational nature. The Grammar School, of which he was a former pupil, had been absorbed into the new **High School**; until the Education Act of 1872 this was the only provider of secondary education in the city, and Harris in his even-handed way resolved to benefit the new school as well as to remedy the shortage of subsidised secondary school places in Dundee. Accordingly in 1874 he

71

gave £20,000 to his old school and £10,000 to build a new academy which was to be named after him. After a long wrangle between the School Board and the High School Corporation, Harris Academy opened in 1885.

Harris died in 1883; shortly afterwards his unmarried sister gave £16,000 to the High to build the Girls' School in Euclid Crescent. In view of the keen rivalry which there was, then and later, between 'The High' and 'The Harris' (definite articles are customary in Dundee usage) it is well to re-member that these two schools were intended to be complementary, and that in fact the former received almost three times as much of the Harris fortune as did the latter. The High had the initial advantage of a central location in the city, thus freeing it from any zoning function, and also a splendid new neo-classical building (see **Reform Street**); the original Harris on the other hand was a second-rate building on a restricted site just off Perth Road at the bottom of Park Place (the site now occupied by the Univerity's Bonar Hall). The school moved in 1926 further west along Perth Road into a magnificent building on a split-level site on the old Blackness escarpment above the river. The 'New Harris' building has been the school's home for seventy years; for a time it was supplemented by the acquisition of the former Logie school as an annexe, but extensions that are planned for the main building will shortly make this arrangement unnecessary.

The Harris traditionally served the western part of the city, as the **Morgan** did the east (there are now several additional schools to serve the northern suburbs); both were and are no-nonsense middle-of-the-road establishments giving a good general education and providing first class candidates for entry into tertiary education. The fee-paying **High** tended to attract mainly the children of wealthier parents; its great debt to William Harris and his sister is not always remembered.

The ex-bailie and former baker, whose benefactions also included funds to establish the Harris chair of Physics in the University, might have been mildly surprised at the different ways in which his educational protégés developed, but he would surely be touched by the reverence in which the name of Harris is still held in Dundee.

Hawkill and West Port

The present Hawkhill is a nondescript ring road leading from West Marketgait to the **Sinderins**. On the pre-1960 maps it can be clearly seen as a westward extension of the **Overgate**. The vestige that remains is called on the present-day map 'Old Hawkhill', and leads from nowhere to no-where; in addition there is now a 'New Hawkhill' which traverses the Blackness Industrial Estate, resumes the line of the Old Hawkhill at Bellfield

Street and veers south to join the Perth Road at the Sinderins.

The transition from Overgate to the old Hawkhill involved negotiating the West Port, originally the historic gateway to the mediaeval town, but later the name of a short street connecting Tay Street with Old Hawkhill. The exact site of the old Port is not known, but is thought to have been south-east of the present roundabout, near Long Wynd (see **Overgate**); it was one of the principal gates of the burgh, controlling all access to and from the west, and was doubtless the route taken by Wallace when making his escape to the Carse of Gowrie (see **Wallace**). The date of the Port is also unknown, but it had apparently become ruinous by 1591 and was ordered by the Provost, Bailies and Town Council to 'be anew repairit in maist honest manner'. It came into prominence again during the Montrose campaign in 1644, and suffered severe damage at the hands of General Monck in the following year. The Port was widened in 1668 and finally demolished in 1757 as being 'a great inconvenience or nuisance to all entereing at this quarter of the town' (was a similar excuse put forward for the demolition of the Royal Arch two centuries later?).

The original Hawk Hill, when it was still open country, may have acquired its name from birds, possibly from association with the aristocratic sport of falconry. The 'hill' is still identifiable (just) as the rising ground behind Belmont Hall of Residence. But the Hawkhill cannot claim the same antiquity as the West Port: unlike Blackness and 'Diddop' its name does not appear on seventeenth-century maps, and it seems to have been part of the estate of Blackness. An old building at the West Port (the one with the clock) was said to mark the site of the barns of Blackness, erected by the first Hunter laird around 1750 (see **Blackness**). The name of Hunter Street (a continuation of Small's Wynd) commemorates the Blackness connection.

The map of 1776 shows a mansion house of 'Haukhill', standing in extensive grounds to the east of Springfield; but shortly thereafter Hawkhill grew (like the Hilltown) as a weaving colony, being described at the time as 'a village near Dundee'. When the land was extensively built over at the beginning of the industrial era, the Hawkhill lost its sport-and-country sound and became the name of a busy street occupied by poor dwellings, shops and linen factories. In fact, the Hawkhill was always rather a mean place, lacking the picturesqueness of the Overgate and the gentility of settlements like nearby Seafield, Westfield and Springfield, where by the mid-nineteenth century an area once occupied by country villas was evolving into a middle-class suburb. Westfield Place remains a good example of Dundee's unpretentious Victorian past.

In the good (or bad) old days, when people actually *lived* in the centre of

Dundee, the Hawkhill was familiarly known as 'The Hackie', just as Blackness Road was 'The Blackie'. After traversing the West Port a favourite stroll was 'up the Hackie an' doon the Blackie': nobody would now make that journey without fear of bodily injury from fast traffic or danger of carbon-monoxide poisoning.

High School

Dundee High School came into existence in the mid-nineteenth century through the amalgamation of three older educational establishments, namely the Grammar School, the Academy and the English school. The Grammar School was a mediaeval church foundation in the vicinity of St Mary's, intended as a training for the priesthood; its buildings were destroyed by the English during the sack of the city in 1548, but a few years later it was rebuilt on a new site (the one presently occupied by the City Square) and as an institution it somehow survived the Reformation. The other two were more recent foundations, both insignificant fee-paying establishments, with only two or three masters each; the Academy's curriculum was of a practical nature, while the so-called English school provided an elementary education. For a time after amalgamation the schools were known collectively as Dundee Public Seminaries, but in 1859 a royal charter established the Corporation of the High School of Dundee as the governing body of the school.

The High School was based on a concept of comprehensive provision of secondary education; and the building, part of a grand plan to dignify Dundee's centre (see **Reform Street**) was erected at an expense of about £10,000—a lot of money in those days. A contemporary writer describes it as being '…in the Doric style of architecture, …its portico…copied from the exquisite model of the Parthenon of Athens…A double-columned gateway, closed in by an iron-palisadoed wall which encircles a beautiful shrubbery, leads to the principal entrance.' Sad to say, the 'beautiful shrubbery' gave way at first to a gravelled playground and latterly to a car park, thus destroying to some extent the original conception; but presumably the school authorities had to move with the times.

Originally the Girls' High School was a separate entity, accommodated in a building on the west side of Euclid Crescent (an inspired name for this street). Built in 1889 in the French style, it is still referred to by pupils as 'the Girls' School' although the two schools have now been integrated for more than half a century. One recalls the imposing stairway, and the hall whose frieze bore the names of what were, according to contemporary standards of taste, the great composers of the time—Auber, Bellini and Donizetti.

Redecoration has deprived today's pupils of this edifying reminder of their cultural heritage.

Dundee High School now enjoys the highest reputation it has ever had, attracting pupils from a wide area and from varying backgrounds. It was from the first an elitist establishment: the official Dundee guide-book of 1878 unashamedly claims that 'ever since its opening [DHS] has been patronised by mostly all the nobility and gentry in and around Dundee'. It is doubtful if such a claim was ever valid, and certainly for most of the present century the school has had a solidly middle-class clientele. But in the immediate post-war years (one speaks from youthful memory) it tended to be pretentious in its self-perception as an ancient institution, maintaining tenuous claims to have among its *alumni* such notable Scots as William Wallace (see **Wallace**) and the historian Hector Boece (who had both in fact attended the Grammar School). It had a great sense of style and took immense pride in such things as its kilted cadet force and its Latin school song; its *esprit de corps* was genuine, if perhaps somewhat artificially induced. These features were no doubt harmless enough, but the school tended to be perceived by less privileged youngsters in the city as a resort for the snobbish. They would refer to its pupils as 'Heh Schule bums'; (*bum* in Dundee colloquially meant 'swank', not anything more vulgar). More importantly, the High School's somewhat dilettante approach to learning at that time did not always provide the solid grounding required for those proceeding to further education; and career guidance was a quite unknown concept.

In the past few decades the High School's academic attainments and enhanced reputation have greatly increased its power to attract good pupils from outside the city. Before then the school's recognised 'catchment area' comprised greater Dundee (including Monifeith, Newport and Tayport); but nowadays pupils are to be seen commuting in quantity from places as distant as St Andrews.

The school used to be the subject of an interesting and informal arrangement in social engineering: each year at the end of Form 2 several pupils (mainly boys) would be removed by their parents to embark on a boarding-school education. The parental motives for this no doubt included social advancement, but the main reason was to assist the boys involved to secure a university place at Oxbridge. The changed pattern of university admission, combined with the school's greater academic prestige, has made this practice all but obsolete. But in any event the departure of these privileged youngsters was more than offset by the annual influx into Form 1 of bursary pupils from the local council primary schools, resulting in great benefit to the school's ethos; at one time there were more than a hundred of these bursars, and without this leavening the High would have been a much less lively establishment. It is to be hoped that an equivalent system of assisted places continues to operate.

Hilltown

The name Hilltown means exactly what you would think—the place or farm on the hill. At an earlier date its full name was Hilltown of Dudhope; that is to say, it was not within the envelope of the mediaeval burgh but was a distinct settlement with a life of its own. Its early development was due to the fact that it lay outside the Wellgait Port (see **Wellgate**) and formed the principal access to the north. It became an important thoroughfare which, as invariably happens, generated further settlement, termed by earlier historians 'the Rotten Row'. It has been claimed that the name is from *rotteram* —'to muster'—denoting 'a place whereat the inhabitants of the neighbouring town assembled in arms' (which would also fit the Rotten Row in Hyde Park), but is more likely to be connected with the Scots word *rottan*, indicating rat-infestation. The strategic position of Dudhope's Hilltown further enhanced its importance, and it was always a prime target for strategists (they included Montrose and Claverhouse) who had designs on Dundee itself.

There exists a charming drawing of Dundee from the east by Slezer done about 1670; the burgh is shown as a small settlement along the shore, while the surroundings are of meadows, woods and hills. The Hilltown (the definite article is obligatory) appears as a ribbon development to the east of the Law, still in the deep countryside. It was described a century later as 'vastly lightsome, having a fore view, it lying so high, and the inhabitants have as much fresh air as if they were a number of miles in the country'. Because of the steepness of the slope, the houses (usually thatched, with adjoining kailyard) were built with their gables to the street, on long rigs which formed horizontal terraces; and although the early development of the Hilltown was totally unplanned, the subsequent layout of courts and wynds tended to conform to this pattern.

Small traders began to thrive in the Hilltown; in particular the weavers and clothmakers were so successful in their manufacturing and marketing arrangements as to threaten the livelihood of their competitors in Dundee, and there was something of a trade war between the two groups. Also of great significance were the bonnetmakers, who throve on the local wool supply; but they in turn succumbed to competition from the west of Scotland; so numerous and important were the practitioners of this ancient craft that Bonnethill was at one time an alternative name for the Hilltown (it is commemorated in Bonnethill church and the modern Bonnethill Court).

The inhabitants of the Hilltown being exempt from the trading restrictions of the burgh of Dundee, there developed a strong rivalry between the craftsmen of the respective places. This trade war became so vexatious that in 1643 a charter by Charles I in favour of Sir James Scrymgeour, 2nd Constable of Dundee and 2nd Viscount Dudhope, elevated the Hilltown into a burgh of barony. The privileges of 'the Barronie' (yet another name for the Hilltown) were thereby formalised, and the influence of an already powerful family increased (see **Scrymgeour**). The new status required that the Hilltown should have its own Baron's Court and Tolbooth (a building which is long demolished but which stood at the foot of the hill), and the charter gave the inabitants certain trading rights within the burgh.

The Town purchased the Barronie in 1697, the estate of Dudhope passed to the municipality in 1705, and baronial jurisidictions disappeared after the Rising of 1745; the office of Constable of Dundee was allowed to lapse, and the separate status of the Hilltown gradually subsided into that of a suburb. With the coming of the industrial era, and the erection of rows of tenements for the incoming workers, the Hilltown of semi-rural landholdings and cottage industries disappeared for ever and became in Victorian times a depressed area described by a contemporary writer as having 'a motley and grotesque appearance, and, though the seat of very extensive manufactures, consists generally of ill-built houses, confusedly interspersed with cloth factories'. In the post-industrial period the area is undergoing further development of a residential kind, and it may be that it will yet return to its former 'lightsome state'.

The Howff

Dervorguilla, Lady of Galloway, was the granddaughter of David earl of Huntingdon and mother of King John Balliol. She is remembered mainly for three benevolent foundations in a life devoted to good works: Sweetheart Abbey near Dumfries, Balliol College in Oxford and the Franciscan house of Greyfriars in Dundee. Professor Douglas Young used to speculate wistfully on what might have been the state of university education in mediaeval Scotland had the Lady Devorguilla done the latter two things the other way round.

Little is known about the Greyfriars monastery apart from the fact that its church and convent were of some magnificence and occupied a site where the Howff now is. In 1310 it was the venue for a significant assembly of the Scottish clergy, who came out in support of Robert the Bruce. But the monastery had an unhappy history: after surmounting severe financial problems it was destroyed by an invading English force in 1547, and the advent of the Reformation some twelve years later meant that it was never restored. Its orchards and arable lands, stretching up to Chapelshade, continued to be cultivated by the friars for some years; but in 1559 the Council claimed the crop and in the following year started recycling the stones of Greyfriars to build a new abattoir and tolbooth for the town. So matters stood until in 1562 Mary Queen of Scots granted a licence to the town 'to bury their deid in that Place and yaird whilk some time wes occupyet by the Gray Cordelier Friars'.

Queen Mary was activated by considerations of public health, for the Greyfriars site, unlike the previous burial ground at St Clement's church, was outwith the town wall; and apparently they ordered these things better in France, where Mary had been raised. But from the beginning it appears, surprisingly, that the new burial ground became a place of resort for the Trades. It is usually explained that it was from this circumstance that the place got its present name of The Howff; and it is true that in Scots the word *howff* means a meeting-pace, nowadays very often a pub. But in fact the representatives of the incorporated trades had previously done their business in the courtyard of the old Greyfriars; and *howff* has the primary meaning of courtyard—indeed it is cognate with German *Hof*, meaning 'court'.

However that may be, the new burial ground proved to be highly satisfactory in its dual capacity, and the various trades appropriated parts of the cemetery for their exclusive use. The weavers designated a spot at the north wall as their particular patch; and when the Nine Trades were instituted in 1581 they paid the Town Council an annual rent for the privilege of meeting at 'the Stone'. One hopes that there were adequate wet-weather arrangements, for it was not until almost 200 years later that the entrepreneurs acquired their own Trades Hall in the High Street (demolished in the 1870s in the interests of street-widening). The Howff was closed as a burial ground in 1867, no doubt having reached the point of saturation.

It is something of a miracle that 'a gruesome derelict cemetery' (as the late James Cameron described the Howff) should have escaped the mass destruction visited on central Dundee in the sixties. It is as though it had been forgotten (which it probably had, although superstition about grave-desecration may have helped to save it); in any event it remains a singular memorial to the mediaeval town. For those with a taste for funerary ornamentation the Howff is a fascinating place, and contains the graves of many of Dundee's celebrated citizens of past eras, with a range of armorial blazons hardly to be equalled in Scotland. The west wall (recently restored) with its ancient archway and arcades is of interest, as is the south wall, which formed part of the defensive boundary of the old town.

The Howff is now maintained by Dundee's Parks Department, and in springtime it has a brave show of bulbs and blossom. Surrounded by office buildings in the centre of the city, and graced with mature trees including (appropriately) some weeping ash, it provides a useful lung; yet it is not easy to see how the Howff can be used to good effect as an amenity for the general public. On fine summer days office-workers from round about come here to lunch *al fresco*, but in winter it can be a dreich place without even the macabre atmosphere of London's Highgate Cemetery or even of Edinburgh's Greyfriars. Again, although the grave-inscriptions are in themselves fascinating, the poor quality of stone which was used adds to the air of desolation. A place in which to contemplate the transience of worldly things rather than to foregather for business or pleasure.

Keiller

If there was ever any validity in the old slogan 'Dundee for jute, jam and journalism', then James Keiller must have been largely responsible for the second component. Keillers is certainly one of the great Dundee traditions, and although the firm is no longer extant the name is still part of the household vocabulary wherever civilised values are maintained.

Like all great legends, the Keiller one has several variants. Was it really Great-aunt Margaret Keiller who devised the perfect recipe for marmalade; or was it an improvisation by Janet Keiller who was already a dab hand at quince jam and had been asked by her husband to find a use for a cargo of bitter Seville oranges? What is certain is that Dundee marmalade became a success story in the early nineteenth century and that its popularity has never diminished despite competition from numerous rivals. At one time this preserve was referred to in France as 'le Dundee'; and marmalade has overshadowed Keiller's jam and other goodies which were just as sought-after in their day.

James Keiller founded a confectionery business in Dundee in 1797 with small capital, with contacts which were at first no more than local, and with no very great commercial aspirations. When he established a monopoly of the new 'Dundee Marmalade', James's business began to proper; in 1820 he assumed his son as a partner (hence 'James Keiller & Son'); and when the founder's grandson John joined the firm in or around 1870 it really took off. John Keiller, a business man with advanced ideas, installed modern machinery and adopted the latest techniques in production and marketing. He was also something of a connoisseur of the arts and a considerable local benefactor.

Under the leadership of John Keiller, and despite various setbacks including punitive import duties on sugar (which necessitated the temporary removal of the factory to Guernsey), and two disastrous fires in the London factory, the firm continued to expand. After the loss of a third factory in the Blitz, Keillers concentrated their post-war manufacturing activities in Dundee; the acquisition in 1947 of a factory in Mains Loan looked after the production of Dundee cake and shortbread, while a new factory on a seven-acre site in Maryfield was responsible for the production of marmalade and Toblerone (previously made in London). These developments seemed to set the seal on the firm's prosperity.

But the inexorable forces of competition were at work and the days of this family firm were numbered; in 1951 Keillers was acquired by a multiple, shortly to be taken over by another, in dog-eat-dog manner, and eventually closed in 1992. The remnants of the business were taken over by an African family, who made a go of the marmalade side of it, before selling out to an English confectioner. So you will look in vain for the name Keiller in the business section of the Dundee telephone directory, apart from that of the Keiller Centre in Chapel Street, near the site of the original Keillers works. Any Keiller delivery vans that you may see are just survivors of the takeover; and although since 1989 the manufacture of fudge, boilings and chocolate has continued in Maryfield (in a works which is open to the public and popular with youngsters), the business is now that of Shaws Dundee Sweet Factory.

Many will remember the old Keillers mill between Albert Square and the High Street, now occupied by the Forum Shopping Centre; when the factory 'skailed' each day and the girls streamed out into New Inn Entry, shouting and laughing and smoking cigarettes, it was like the opening scene of the opera *Carmen* (except that there weren't often fights). Remember also the pleasant Keiller tearooms overlooking the City Square, which always seemed to be full of sunshine. Despite all the changes we can't forget the part played by this firm in a century and a half of Dundee's history.

The name itself is not without interest. Commoner in Dundee and Angus than anywhere else (with its alternative spelling of Keillor), it was the surname of a landed family as long ago as the thirteenth century. Originally it would be a place-name, as in Inverkeilor in the Mearns and Keillor near Coupar Angus; it means 'hard water' and is a variant of the name Calder. But to the rest of the world, Keiller means marmalade and Dundee cake.

King's Cross

The word cross turns up frequently in place-names. Sometimes it merely refers to crossroads, as in Crossgates in Fife; sometimes to a market cross,

80

as in Fishcross and Mearns Cross. Dundee's King's Cross has a much more interesting history, and one that is unknown to the vast majority of its citizens. To arrive at the derivation of the name, we must ignore the presence of the hospital, and look westwards to Pitalpin Street at the point where Liff Road meets the Kingsway; we must indeed look further back in time to a period (perhaps a century and a half ago) when King's Cross and Pitalpin were in the deep countryside.

Alpin is of course a personal name, but nobody seems to know exactly who he was; although there is an Alpin in the early Celtic king-list, it is by no means certain that the Alpin who was the father of Kenneth mac Alpin was indeed of the royal blood. Our knowledge of the period (early to midtenth century) comes almost entirely from the mediaeval chronicles, written many years later and by scholars who were intent on reinforcing the legendary antiquity of Scottish kingship; but since this is all the knowledge we have or are likely to have, there is no harm in repeating the chroniclers' version of the story, which runs as follows: Alpin, king of the Scots, was in conflict with Brude, king of the Picts, and despite the heroic resistance of the former, it was the Picts who carried the day. Alpin was successfully defending his position on the north-western slopes of the Law, and had all but turned the course of the battle when the Pictish camp-followers, coming over the brow of the hill at Clatto, convinced the Scots that they were outnumbered and put them to flight. (This is a familiar enough motif in Scotland's story.) Alpin was then taken prisoner by the Picts and beheaded at the command of their king.

The best evidence that we have of all this is from the place-names. Pitalpin means simply 'the place of Alpin', and the name was probably coined after the putative date of the battle (943) and some time before the writing of the chronicles some two centuries later. It probably does not, as the guidebooks used to maintain, mean 'grave of Alpin' for there was at one time a village of Pitalpin; and in any case, *pit* means 'piece' and not 'grave' (see **Introduction**). Pitalpin village is described in the 1860s as lying about three miles to the west of the city, on a site which by then had come to be occupied by a nursery. Since most of the nineteenth century landmarks have disappeared, this site is difficult to locate but was probably around the south-east corner of the Camperdown policies, near the former Dryburgh farm (which in turn gave its name to various new streets in the vicinity).

Tradition has it that the place of Alpin's execution was King's Cross, but the exact location of that spot is even more difficult to determine. In the nineteenth century there was a property known as King's Cross Cottage, some 500 yards to the east of Pitalpin village, and it was at that time possible to identify the place where a cross had been erected; it was apparently at a bend at the foot of the present King's Cross Road. King's Cross Hospital was built in the late nineteenth century as an 'epidemic' institution, and no doubt took its name from the existing road; the buildings would lie on the outskirts of the city, as befitted a fever hospital. If one mentally eliminates the urban developments between King's Cross Road and Camperdown East Lodge, it becomes clear that as the crow flies Alpin's place of execution must have been not far from the battlefield.

The naming of Macalpine Road to the north is of course much later, and a bit far-fetched, unless one assumes that Alpin was indeed the father of Kenneth mac Alpin who is generally reckoned to be the first monarch of the new kingdom that came to be known as Scotland.

Kinloch

This familiar Gaelic place-name element means 'at the head of the lake' (in Scots, 'Lochhead') and occurs all over the Highlands, usually in conjunction with a more specific name, as in Kinlochbervie. (The fact that Kinloch Rannoch is at the *foot* of the loch must be regarded as a linguistic blip). Sometimes the name appears in places where there is no loch to be seen, as in Kinloch near Collessie in North East Fife: there was once a loch here, with the hamlet of Kinloch at its head, but modern agricultural drainage methods have made the area dry.

It is this insignificant little place which gave its name—in a somewhat indirect way—to a very gifted Dundee family. Nothing is known of the origin of the Kinlochs, but from the twelfth century they held estates in Collessie parish and (when surnames became the order of the day) called themselves after their property. The family appears to have been dispossessed of their Kinloch property in the reign of James II, but at the beginning of the seventeenth century acquired other lands in Angus. In this case the lands (having been elevated into a barony) were named after the family and not *vice versa*; although this practice was uncommon in Scotland there are one or two other examples, as in the nearby estate of Fotheringham, named after an Anglo-Norman family which had emigrated from Northamptonshire in the fourteenth century. So Kinloch came to be the name of an estate which boasts no loch but is pleasantly situated to the south of the River Isla, a mile or so west of Meigle on the A94. The Adam-style mansion (which in 1797 replaced an earlier one) now houses an antiques business.

It is the family however which was important in Dundee. The story starts in a humble enough manner: the Kinlochs through several generations held the post of Parish Clerk, the duties attaching to which included the maintenance of the town 'knok' (clock) and its chimes. Another member of the family was Treasurer of the town. By the 1550s the Kinlochs had come to play a leading part in Dundee's mercantile affairs, trading extensively in foreign ports, especially the Baltic. William Kinloch prospered sufficiently to acquire property known as 'Kinloch's Meadow' on what is now part of Albert Square (see **Meadows**); his actual residence was at the foot of what later became Union Street, then a quiet riverside retreat.

The first really distinguished Kinloch was David, born about 1560, who turned out to be a true Renaissance man, making his name as physician, courtier, diplomat and poet. He is known to have matriculated at St Andrews University in 1576 (as an Arts student, for medical studies did not become available there for more than another two hundred years). He graduated M.D. at a continental university (possibly Paris or Reims) and is thought to have been at one time physician to the French Royal Family. He was certainly 'Mediciner to His Majestie' (James VI) from 1597 and undertook important diplomatic missions for the king. One of these involved a visit to Spain, and when diplomacy failed he was imprisoned in Madrid; a family story goes that he won a reprieve by writing a prescriptive cure for the Grand Inquisitor's fever and attaching it to the tail of the prison cat. Kinloch was also noted as the author of a quantity of Latin verse on some of the medical aspects of human reproduction, much valued by medical historians. He became a burgess of Dundee in 1602 and his tomb is still to be seen in the **Howff**.

The family's subsequent activities were no less enterprising. During the eighteenth century they were committed Jacobites, and turned out in numbers in both of the Risings; Sir James Kinloch raised the second batallion of the Forfarshire regiment in 1746 (and as a result of his enthusiasm ended his days in exile). By the following century they seem to have abandoned their Royalist leanings, and the most celebrated member of the family, George Kinloch of Kinloch, earned for himself the title of 'the Radical Laird'. Born in Dundee in 1775, he spent part of his youth in France where he absorbed some of the current egalitarian ideals, and in 1819 he addressed a large popular assembly on the **Magdalen** Green in terms that officialdom considered too inflammatory; he was charged with sedition and when he fled to France to escape trial he was outlawed *in absentia* for 'the advocacy of popular rights'. There is little doubt that Kinloch was victimised more for betrayal of his class (he was a landowner and a J.P.) than for his reforming ideas; and although he was later pardoned and eventually elected as member for Dundee in the first reformed parliament, his health was broken and he died a year later. In addition to his political activities he had for long interested himself in Dundee's civic affairs including the development of the **Docks** and of the Dundee-Newtyle railway line (on which he was doubtless an occasional commuter). Fifty years after his election as MP his statue was erected in Albert Square to 'commemorate a signal triumph of political justice'; it is still there, in between Rabbie Burns and Victoria Regina—but nobody seems nowadays to pay much attention to this, the city's one and only tribute to George Kinloch, one of Dundee's more distinguished citizens.

Kinnaird

For any middle-aged Dundonian, the name Kinnaird means a cinema that stood in Bank Street before the demolitions of the 1960s. But it is really much more interesting than that. Built in 1857 as a Corn Exchange, it later became the Kinnaird Hall, a venue for lectures and political meetings. During the visit of the British Association to Dundee in 1867 the hall was thronged with working men anxious to witness the latest scientific discoveries; this led to a series of popular lectures in the hall by people as eminent as T.H. Huxley. On the same occasion the hall was the scene of a 'sumptuous banquet' and 'the most splendid ball that Dundee has yet witnessed' (BA attenders no longer enjoy such frivolities); it was also a venue for concerts and meetings before it became a cinema in the 1920s, when a craze for 'the showies' (later known as 'the pictures') swept Dundee and every suitable auditorium was converted for the purpose. But the Kinnaird, it has to be said, was not a particularly attractive or successful picture emporium. It is now a hole in the ground.

A popular Dundee legend is of Winston Churchill addressing a Liberal party rally there during his unsuccessful campaign of 1922, and of how a suffragette was lowered through the arched roof in order to put him further off his stride. As usual the truth is even more interesting. The Kinnaird Hall was in fact the venue for several political meetings during the era of the suffragettes (including one led by Emmeline Pankhurst herself). The first of these was in 1909 when a public meeting about the Budget had been called. A group of suffragettes had chalked urgent messages on the pavement outside inviting crowd support in their plan to hijack the meeting, and this was so successful that a mob of a thousand people tried to force their way in; chaos ensued when the ladies found themselves pushed by the crowd from behind and barred by the police in front. Several arrests were made for breach of the peace, and the tender-hearted Dundee constabulary apparently found it distasteful to have to restrain such high-minded law-breakers as these young lassies. It is noteworthy that two of the protesters were

Londoners and two were students from the USA: rent-a-suffragette was not uncommon.

The Churchill incident had an altogether more feminine touch than in the legend. The ringleader had spent the entire day on the roof of the Kinnaird Hall, intending to open one of the rooflights and lower herself by a rope; the glass however would not yield to her gentle touch and she had to let herself in through a side window. Her reward was ten days in the slammer, with the possible consolation that she may have contributed to Churchill's defeat.

The Kinnaird Hall was a gift to the city by George, 9th Baron Kinnaird, who was a noted statesman and philanthropist of the mid-nineteenth century. A liberal in politics, he was a great enthusiast for education and agricultural improvement. Lord Kinnaird was the descendant of a family which had held lands in the Carse since the twelfth century: the family title is taken from the village of Kinnaird near Inchture, and Kinnaird Castle was the family seat until the reign of Charles I. The castle was once a place of some importance: it was visited by James VI in 1617—in fact he stayed there for a week. The Kinnairds later acquired through marriage the estate of Inchture, and built Rossie Priory, which remained until recently the family home.

The ninth laird had been ennobled as Lord Kinnaird of Inchture in 1682 (a reward by Charles II for devotion to the royalist cause); prior to that the family were styled simply 'Kinnaird of that Ilk' (that is to say, Kinnaird of Kinnaird). The name Kinnaird used to enjoy great fame in Dundee, and in the 1830s was one of several proposed for the splendid new thoroughfare which was to link the High Street with the Meadows (see under **Constitution** and **Reform**). The noble Lord had to be satisfied with Kinnaird Street on the south slope of the Law. Kinnaird may be no longer a household word with us, but it conjures up memories of the city that was.

Kirkton

Kirkton High School was the first comprehensive school to be built in Dundee after the war; *in* Dundee may seem not quite the right term, for the school buildings are right on the northern perimeter, near Harestane Road and several miles from its nearest rival, the Morgan Academy, whose catchment area used to comprise the north-eastern part of the city. After some teething troubles, Kirkton High has now established itself as a successful purveyor of secondary education for the area with a small but regular supply of pupils for tertiary education.

But how did it get its name? From the small village of Kirkton which occupied a site at Downfield and which at the beginning of the nineteenth century consisted of a kirk, a manse, a school and schoolhouse and three or four cottages. Of the early settlement only the manse now remains, the rest having been swallowed up in the Victorian suburb of Downfield. Indeed it is not easy nowadays to locate the old village of Kirkton, but it must have been roughly where Kirkton Road joins Strathmartine Road.

There is more to the name than that, however. The oldest type of settlement in historic Scotland (if we ignore the Pictish and earlier eras) consisted of a few houses grouped round a kirk—hence 'kirk toun', of which a very early example is Monifieth (although it was never so-named). There must have at one time been hundreds of these Kirktons, but very often the term 'Kirkton' served as a prefix to another name: an example would be Kirkton of Tealing, which just became 'Tealing'. Another is Kirkton of Monikie, which is a good mile from the village of that name, and yet another is Kirkton of Airlie, which is now just plain 'Airlie'. Sometimes both kirk and settlement failed to survive, leaving Kirkton as a farm name.

Our Kirkton must originally have been the kirk-toun of something-or-other—but of what? The nearest village, Kirkton of Strathmartine, is two miles to the north, and had its own church and school. Not, surely, 'Kirkton of Downfield', for Downfield would originally have been a field-name and not a settlement-name, and the place did not grow to any size until the coming of the Caledonian Railway in the mid-nineteenth century. It would be interesting to have the correct (or even a plausible) answer—not that the matter is of the smallest practical importance.

Law and Sidlaw

Law is one of the most frequently-found hill names on the map of Lowland Scotland, and usually occurs in conjunction with a local settlement-name—examples are Largo Law and Berwick Law. As a common noun, *law* (an Anglo-Saxon term for a rounded hill) is no longer in common use, so that we have frequent references to 'law hills', which of course is saying the same thing twice. In Dundee, the term 'the Law Hill' is often heard, especially in semi-official usage; 'Dundee Law' is more formal. But your true-born Dundonian will usually say 'the Law' (it did not attain its capital letter until the 1850s); and the children's hide-and-seek jingle gives the old pronunciation—'Come oot, come oot, wherever ye are, although ye're at the back o' the La'.

The Law is nowadays in the geographical centre of the Dundee conurbation, but was of course well outside the confines of the mediaeval burgh; consequently it played a relatively minor part in the early history of the city. There is unmistakable evidence of a vitrified Iron Age defensive fort on the top of the Law, and there are indications that the summit was re-fortified by the Romans in the second century AD. Recent excavations have uncovered evidence of the existence of an earthen-walled citadel, presumed to have been constructed around the mid-sixteenth century when an English army was laying siege to Dundee from **Broughty** castle. There has been some flattening of the summit over the centuries, most of it having taken place during the past seventy years in connection with the construction of an access road and the erection of a war memorial and a transmitter station.

The Law formed part of the large estate of **Dudhope**, portions of which were feued for housing in the nineteenth century. It goes without saying that it was completely unbuilt-on before then. A Gazetteer of 1848 describes the Law as being 'cultivated up its whole ascent, till it shoots into a round, green and unusually pleasing summit'; the last bit is still true, but there is more evidence now on the lower slopes of housing than of cultivation, apart from the traditional allotments and a bit of recent afforestation on the north. A tarmac road goes all the way to the summit, which is dominated by a massive memorial to Dundee's dead of two world wars. A far cry from the days when Dundee lassies used to go there to wash their faces on May morning.

The Law is the source of several other Dundee names: the builders on the western slopes pre-empted the name Lawside, giving Lawside Road and Terrace, and Lawside School, once the only Roman Catholic academy in the city, but now one among three. Law Crescent on the north is descriptive of a road that follows the round contours, while the new Law Road leads to the car park below the summit. Inverlaw is however a contradiction in terms, since *inver* is the Gaelic term for a river-mouth or confluence; presumably Inverlaw Terrace and Steps were called after the mansion of that name on Dudhope Terrace. Inverlaw House belonged to the Halley family (of Wallace Craigie jute works), who must take the blame for this absurd piece of name-giving.

Sidlaw, or the 'Sidlaws' (pronounced 'Seedlies' by Dundee laddies of old) involves the word *law* with a Gaelic prefix—thought to be *suidhe*, meaning 'seat'. So, in modern English, Sidlaws would mean something like 'seat hills', and indeed one of them is called King's Seat. The Sidlaws are a gentle range of hills protecting Dundonians from the northerly blasts, as well as providing a pleasant backdrop when viewed from any angle. They are undervalued, underused and unsung: one of the few mentions they get in Dundee's street-nomenclature is in Sidlaw Avenue in Downfield, although the Sidlaw Group figure in the city's industrial vocabulary. Were the Sidlaws in Derbyshire or Lancashire they would be traversed by a marked footpath from Kinnoul to Kincaldrum, with numerous offshoots leading to signposted pubs in the delightful glens that intersect the range. And there would be adequate public transport at convenient points to and from the city centre. It may come yet, for a' that.

Leng

John Leng was Liberal MP for Dundee, having been elected unopposed in 1889, and holding the seat until shortly before his death in 1906. He was knighted for his services to journalism and public affairs, and resided in affluence in a Victorian Gothic mansion which he built in Newport. The family mausoleum (not many people know this) is the chapel whose grace-ful spire is visible from the A92 Leuchars-Dundee road, adjacent to the green lawns of the new Drumoig golf course. The Leng offices, having in 1851 moved round the corner from the old cramped premises in Argyle Close off the Overgate, came to occupy most of Bank Street; and Leng Street on the east side of the Law was named in his honour.

So why, as the 21st century approaches, should we remember this typi-cal Victorian grandee? In fact, Leng's rise to fame and fortune was not without interest for later generations. A Yorkshireman, he became editor of the *Hull Advertiser* at the early age of nineteen; while still young he bought himself into the *Dundee Advertiser*, which had been launched as a radical bi-weekly in 1801, with a very limited circulation. With the aid of his equally left-wing editor, William Latto, he transformed the newspaper into a flour-ishing daily; and although there can now be few people who remember the old 'Tizer', the paper was one of the component parts of the *Dundee Cou-rier and Advertiser* which came into being through amalgamation after the General Strike of 1926. (See **Thomson**; the title has now been abbreviated to *The Courier*).

Even more noteworthy was Leng's *Peoples Journal*, an odd combina-tion of news, radical views and generally useful practical information; the 'P.J.' attained by 1914 a circulation of over a quarter of a million, making it the largest-selling newspaper outside London; it lasted until 1990 when its demise plunged Dundee into mourning (well, almost). The *People's Friend*, a quasi-literary but cosily sentimental offshoot of the P.J., was popu-larly known as 'The Peeplie'. The *Evening Telegraph*, printed in several editions and circulated over a wide area, still survives, although greatly changed in format and restricted mainly to sales within the city; but alas even in Dundee the once familiar expression 'the Telly' now means some-thing quite different.

Dundee owes a lot to Sir John Leng—and his advocacy of such causes as universal suffrage, anti-imperialism, free education, home rule and land-nationalisation would, one might have imagined, earn him a place in the pantheon of his adopted city. But his name is now remembered in a quite different connection: he was the creator of the Leng Trust, which annually gives some sixty silver and two gold medals for competition among children attending Dundee schools. It is thanks to the beneficence of this versatile Yorkshireman that many Dundee vocalists owe their first introduction to serious music-making; and it is a mark of his magnanimity that 'the subjects of competition must be entirely Scottish'.

Linlathen

This is the name of a pre-war council housing estate, part of what used to be given the unattractive (and often unfair) description of 'slum clearance'. Situated to the north of the Kingsway and to the east of Forfar Road, it was chosen in 1936 as the site of a building scheme of 340 cedar-clad houses; this was at the time in the nature of an experiment (successful as it turned out, and indeed much modern house-building is of timber-frame construction). Linlathen has now grown into a suburb and has settled down into respectability. For a time it had its own High School, but population fluctuations in those of school age have necessitated a merger with Whitfield and a transfer to a new site.

Linlathen (pronounced Lin*lah*-then) is in fact a rather beautiful name, although with a prosaic meaning. It probably comprises the Gaelic words *lann* (an enclosure) and *leathan* (broad), and the total will mean simply 'big field'. Two earlier spellings of the name are Lumbtithen and Lumlethan; these (apart from suggesting a connection with the nearby Ballumbie) appear to be corrupt and are of little help in deciding on the etymology. The name of the Linlathen housing scheme was borrowed from an old estate, which was once in the deep countryside but now lies uncomfortably close to the East Pitkerro Industrial Estate and to the busy Arbroath Road just north of Balgillo.

The early history of the original Linlathen property is not easy to ascertain, beyond the fact that part of it belonged to the earls of Angus. By the seventeenth century it had come into the possession of the Graham family (see **Mains**). The old mansion of Linlathen seems to have been a Graham dower house, or to have been let to tenants as the Graham fortunes declined (which they did, drastically, in the mid-eighteenth century). Robert Graham, 11th laird of Fintry, was in debt to the extent that he could not afford the upkeep of two properties (Mains and Linlathen); he removed his wife to

Fowlis Castle and himself became factor to the Duke of Atholl. (It was from this time on that Mains Castle gradually to fell into ruin.)

The 12th laird, also Robert, born in 1749, was the first and only Graham laird to live in Linlathen; his name was to be seen carved on one of the steading buildings with the dates 1770 and 1771; he probably lived in the mansion for the next decade, where he conducted his well-known friendship with Robert Burns, and was an addressee of some of the poet's verse epistles. Burns was a house-guest from time to time and a window pane in the house is said to have borne the poet's initials with the date 1789. Graham as Commisioner of Excise assisted Burns in obtaining a commission as a guager, thereby relieving his distressed financial condition and probably prolonging his poetic life (see also **Fintry**).

When the Mains estate was rouped in 1787 'for the benefit of his creditors', Robert Graham lived again at Linlathen for a short time, and then sold up to Sir John Stirling, who added a wing to the early Georgian house of the Grahams. The estate was then acquired by the Erskines of Mains Castle (see **Mains**); they occupied Linlathen for many years and had Thomas Carlyle as a frequent guest; (they incidentally gave the family name to Erskine Street in Dundee).

Linlathen House had the dubious distinction of being one of the few properties in the Dundee area which engaged the attention of the Luftwaffe. Just after midnight on Friday 2 August 1940 a German aircraft (presumably intent on shedding its load before returning over the North Sea) dropped twenty-three 50Kg bombs around the house. The whole building shook, plaster fell from the ceilings, windows were blown in—but the only casualty was a cat which apparently had no business to be there in the first place.

Linlathen was occupied during the Second World War by Polish and other troops. The original Graham mansion-house fell into dilapidation and had to be demolished in 1958; the Stirling wing survived for another twenty-five years, being all that remained of the original buildings (apart from the steading built by Robert Graham in 1770). The Linlathen site was completely bulldozed in 1990 and the mansion replaced by a cheerful and bustling Nursing Home, incorporating a Young Disabled Unit. The policies retain something of their former charm, and although the once-noble trees are showing signs of decrepitude, the Dighty Water still flows merrily past on its way to the sea. And it is heartening to see the avenues and the grounds being enjoyed by patients and their carers.

Lochee

On the north-eastern edge of the estate of Invergowrie (see **Gowrie**) there was a hamlet with the unappealing name of Backside of Invergowrie; it had begun to grow in the 1730s, and until recently some dilapidated cottages in Yeaman's Alley (near Lochee Primary School) remained as part of the original settlement. In the early nineteenth century when the property came into the hands of the **Cox** family there developed a flourishing hand-weaving industry with bleachfields, utilising the resources of the Mile End burn. The burn had its source in a water-hole called Loch Eye (long-vanished), and its name was adopted, in the spelling Lochee, as that of the fast-expanding village. (Lochee was not even in the Dundee postal area: delivery of a letter destined for 'Anderson's Lane, South Road, Lochee, Scotland' and postmarked 28 December 1879 was unavoidably delayed by one day, not because of inadequate addressing—it had spent a night on the river bed, having been caught up in the Tay Bridge disaster.)

By this time the Cox business enterprises had flourished to such an extent that the little village had become an important linen manufacturing centre; and with the introduction of steam-powered weaving in 1845 Lochee became virtually a Cox company town. (Evidence of this can still be seen at the bend in the centre of Lochee, where the entrance to the factories led directly off the High Street near the clock-towered East Church which was demolished in the 1960s). By the mid-nineteenth century, when jute had come into its own, Camperdown Works (see under **Camperdown**) had become a vast one-company industrial estate; and when the need for additional personnel became apparent Cox Brothers ran up cheap housing for the workers to the west of their property.

Lochee was well outside the burgh limits until almost the present century, and the journey thither involved passing through the lands of **Logie**, negotiating the 'den' between Balgay Hill and the Law, and climbing to the heathland—reckoned to be hazardous for pedestrians on account of the footpads who roamed the area. In later days the outward journey from the town centre was possibly even worse: 'Lochee—nae licht !' used to be a familiar complaint, a reference to the inadequacy of the gas lighting system. The press with greater restraint and decorum talked about 'the dark suburb'.

The Coxes recruited large amounts of Irish labour, and the population of Lochee grew by a factor of four in the decade following 1840. For a time it had the reputation of being a wild and lawless place: various tenements in South Road were known as Tipperary and The Bog, where unofficial structural alterations were put in hand by the occupants to enable them to transfer from one house to another in the event of unwelcome attention from the forces of law and order. Such, at any rate was local legend, no doubt greatly exaggerated; Irish immigration was certainly a very important element in

Dundee's social history, but in few other cities has integration been so complete or successful.

There was a great degree of interdependence between the workforce and Cox Brothers: Cox needed the labour, and the workers needed the wages and the housing, however poor, that went with the job. The Cox family in fact became local benefactors; they presented Lochee park to the town and endowed a chair of Anatomy in University College (as it then was) as well as building a public library and swimming baths in Lochee. But Lochee was renowned for its militancy, which reached a climax in the great strike of 1923, when the employees at the Camperdown Works were out for a total of 27 weeks. Thereafter the aggressive trade unionism of the immediate post-war years diminished, to be followed by the depression of the 1930s and the slide to war.

Lochee used to have a character of its own, with a High Street containing shops, banks and a parish church, not to speak of a railway station (on the Blairgowrie line) as well as the above-mentioned public baths and a wash-house erected in memory of Thomas Hunter Cox of Maulesden and Strathmartine (see **Cox**); there was even, around the turn of the century, a flourishing Literary Association. And if Lochee's immediate surroundings were sordid, the road to the west had pleasant scenery which was well within walking distance. Local amenities had improved too with the creation of Lochee Park in 1899. The suburb underwent a by-pass operation in the 1960s, whereby the High Street was first marginalised and then transfigured so as to conform to the often deplorable taste of that decade. More recently, Stack Park (created out of part of the Camperdown works site and named after the chimney—see under **Cox**) has become a vast shopping centre and also houses much of modern Dundee's entertainment industry. All has changed; but older readers will remember with nostalgia the distinctive tram (known as 'the car') which ran with great regularity and dependability up Tay Street, past Dudhope and out the winding road to Lochee.

Logie

This familiar place-name crops up all over Scotland north of the Forth; it comes from the Gaelic *lag*, meaning hollow, and appears in its diminutive form in Laggan. Logie (*logaidh*) shows the word in its locative case and means 'at the hollow'. As is usually the case in Scotland, the surname Logie comes from the place and not vice-versa. (The suggestion that the name Lochee may share the same etymology as Logie may be discounted—see **Lochee**.)

The lands of Logie are shown on Crawford's map of Dundee (1793) as being an extensive estate lying to the north of Blackness, with a plain two-storied mansion set in ornamental grounds. A less old map shows the mansion to have occupied a quadrilateral formed by the present Lochee Road, Cleghorn Street, Benvie Road and Mitchell Street; it is impossible nowadays to visualise the terrain, but the house must have had a fine view. The hollow which gave Logie its name would be part of the defile between the Law and Balgay Hill (see **Balgay** and **Lochee**); before the area was built up it used to be referred to as 'Logie Den', where there was a toll-house on the turnpike road to Coupar Angus. The area was drained by the Scourin Burn; a spring which was situated at the present Milnbank Road was known as 'the Logie spout' and in pre-industrial days was responsible for a substantial part of the burgh's water supply. The old Logie church was situated near the present Tullideph Street, which may explain why that part of the Lochee Road appears on the present-day maps as 'Logie Street'—it can never have been part of the original Logie policies.

The southmost portion of the lands of Logie became heavily industrial-ised early in the nineteenth century—no doubt because of the proximity of the Scourin Burn. Logie Works (1828) in Brook Street is one of the oldest surviving factories in Dundee: originally a flax mill, it has always been known by its traditional name of the Coffin Mill. The reason for the nomen-clature is simply the peculiar wedge shape of its inner courtyard, although the building came to be associated in the popular imagination with a fatal accident in which a female employee was dragged by her long hair into the unguarded machinery—an all too common occurrence in the days before employers had statutory responsibility for health and safety at work.

The name Logie now has rather different associations in Dundee. On the lower southern slope of Balgay Hill there was laid out in the 1920s a housing scheme financed by the town council and subsidised by the gov-ernment under various Housing Acts. They called it Logie, although not built on the historic lands of that name; designed by James Thomson, the city architect, it was one of the first municipal housing schemes in Scot-land. Its broad central avenue (named Logie Avenue) gave it a well laid-out appearance, and its leafy side-streets with names such as Sycamore Place and Ashbank Road, added to a sylvan aura which was reinforced by the adjacent Balgay Park. A viewpoint on the high ground to the west gives an impressive vista of the town and the estuary.

Another of the features of the Logie scheme was a new-fangled heating system operated from a central plant; it was said that in cold weather the steam could be seen rising from the street, and it is not surprising that some tenants apparently found their own bit of it too expensive to run. Logie was,

93

and still is a model garden suburb, and it is a pity that financial exigencies (affecting both landlord and tenant) took over; the depression of the thirties, followed by the war, meant that the example set by James Thomson's creation was followed in all too few subsequent corporation housing developments.

Low and Bonar

At the time of the final flowering of the jute industry this combination of names was as well-known in Dundee as Marks & Spencer or Morecambe & Wise. The firm still flourishes in the form 'Low & Bonar PLC, Packaging Plastics, Textiles and Electronics', a good illustration of how heavy industry adapts to modern times. Bonar House is in Faraday Street near the Camperdown Gates and far removed from the satanic mills where the firm originated.

Individually both Low and Bonar may be said to be Dundee names: Low, which originally indicated shortness of stature, has been known in these parts since the fourteenth century, while Bonar ('debonair') was recorded in Dundee at least as long ago as 1554.

The firm was founded in 1902, in order to take over the textile branch of an existing Dundee firm of which John Low had been a partner for many years, and George Bonar was appointed managing director. To begin with it was just a merchandising partnership, which returned to manufacturing in 1909 with the purchase of the East Port calendar. Three years later, with a capital of £500,000 and premises in King Street, it became a limited company. Expansion was rapid; it took over the jute-weaving firm of William Fergusson & Co, and within twenty years had in addition acquired Dudhope Jute Works and the Bank Mills Spinning Company. The big break-through came in 1924 when Low & Bonar acquired **Baxter** Brothers & Co; by this time 'Lobos', as it was familiarly known, controlled, with Jute Industries Ltd, more than half of the city's jute trade. The building of an extension to Baxters' Eagle Jute Mills (1930) with its facade on Victoria Street was the firm's final fling, and the only significant new factory building of that decade; and it was surely a remarkable development at a time when unemployment in the jute trade was fifty per cent.

Low & Bonar moved into engineering in the 1950s and 60s and also took the lead in transferring from jute to polypropylene; they were shortly, along with Tay Textiles and Don Bros Buist, to account for two-thirds of UK polypropylene output. With Sidlaw Industries (the successor to Jute Industries Ltd) Low & Bonar produced 'Polytape', which took them into the packaging sector. So the new Lobos occupies a different, cleaner world from that of jute, and sanitised polypropylene silos have taken the place of the old manufactories, warehouses and sweatshops.

Individually and corporately the Lows and the Bonars have been generous local benefactors. The gift to Dundee of the School of Economics by
George Bonar in the 1930s was a handsome benefaction, although attended
with some difficult constitutional problems. Bonar, anxious to encourage
commercial education above the level of shorthand and typing, had offered
to provide the necessary funds to found a Commercial College which would
become a component part of the University of St Andrews; in those far-off
days the Scottish universities were hidebound by rules (not all of their own
devising) which prescribed strict academic entrance qualifications which
were not in line with Bonar's plans, and the gift had to be declined—a
circumstance which at the time did not bring credit to a university whose
motives, in some Dundee eyes, were already suspect. So the School of
Economics (in Bell Street) was put under the control of the Dundee Education Department, with degrees which were awarded externally. Despite these
cumbersome restrictions, the College flourished, and in 1955 it was brought
under the aegis of the University, to form part of the new Social Science
Faculty in Queen's College. The University of Dundee, after it had come
into its own in 1967, made further amends by naming one of its new buildings Bonar Hall.

McGonagall

This uncommon name is well-known in Dundee (but practically nowhere
else) as that of 'the world's worst poet'. The terminology is both inaccurate
and unjust, for William of that name in no way merited the title of poet: his
writings are totally devoid of any merit whatever, literary or poetic or socio-
historical. If you were to take an average Dundonian and compel him or her
to pen some verses on a notable public event—say the bicentenary of the
battle of Camperdown—the result would probably be no better and no worse
than McGonagall; the difference is that poor simple-minded McGonagall
was under the mistaken belief that his verses were the result of heavenly
inspiration. He was strengthened in this delusion by being subjected to a
series of cruel hoaxes on the part of some of the city's journalistic wits
(who probably were only marginally cleverer than he). The mockery reached
its shameful climax when the wretched man accepted a spoof invitation to
give a poetry-reading before Queen Victoria at Balmoral, only to be shown
the door after his 70-mile tramp across the Cairnwell from Dundee. It cannot be claimed even that McGonagall's verse has any merit as contemporary
reportage; his mind is too commonplace and his powers of expression too
limited for any such thing. The main interest to us nowadays of the doings
of this rhymester is how society could be so cruel as to find humour in the

poor man's fantasies. After a century, the joke has lost any savour it may have had, and poor McGonagall deserves to be forgotten: neither he nor his tormentors have brought any credit to Dundee. William Topaz McGonagall (the middle name was an afterthought) came to Dundee from Edinburgh, and was a weaver in one of the jute mills. He left the city in disillusionment in 1894 when persecution from the street urchins and mockery by the literati became intolerable. Although neither his birth nor his death took place in Dundee, there is no other place which is likely to claim him.

There are still several bearers of the name in the Dundee area, with variants of McGonigle, McGonagle and McGonical. The large variety of spellings should not surprise us, for the name is a reduction of the Irish Gaelic *Mac Congal* (Congal being a personal name, apparently meaning 'of high valour'). The ancestors of the 'poet' would originally have come from Donegal, where the name was noted as that of a family of ecclesiastics; his immediate forebears seem to have come to Scotland as part of the vast immigration of Irish labourers which occurred as a result of the famines of the 1840s (see **Lochee**).

Magdalen Yard

Magdalen as a common noun meant a repentant prostitute, and, as an adjective, refers originally to Mary of Magdala (or the Magdalene) who figures in Luke's gospel. (Maudlin is another spelling of the adjective, but this particular pronunciation is more commonly heard in Oxford than in Dundee). A number of convents and monastic dependancies were called after the Magdalene, and there is a tradition of such a one in the area, probably at the foot of Step Row, where several carved stones were unearthed 150 years ago. The Yard bit is probably from Old English *geard* meaning a yard or garden, although Gaelic had its own word *garradh*, giving many Highland place-names with the element *gart* or *garth*. It usually signified a grassy place, and is found also in Guardbridge in Fife.

Magdalen Yard originally formed part of the shoreline of the Tay estuary, and appears to have been a common meeting ground and place of resort from a very early period. Not only for recreation—during the plague of 1585 the magistrates met there in the open air as a matter of safety, and the Town Council in 1679 at the beginning of the Covenanting wars summoned a rendezvous of all the fencible men of the burgh between sixteen and sixty. The area became one of the first of the Dundee suburbs, with several fine Georgian houses whose gardens ran down to the river, and whose cellars within living memory contained the remains of boats; the foreshore was formed into a public park in the 1840s as part of the effort to create additional employment. The coming of the railway in 1847 brought further changes, mostly unwelcome to the users of the park as the Yard was effectively cut off from the riverfront, making bathing (horrid thought) impossible.

In time large areas of estuary were reclaimed to create the Esplanade and the marshalling yards below Seabraes; the Caledonian (later the LMS) railway line runs along the south of Magdalen Yard, and until the 1940s it was not unusual for local dwellers to commute to the town centre from Magdalen Green railway station. Nevertheless these vast developments, including the bypass road and the airport, do not detract from the magnificent view up-river, and Magdalen Yard Road and its westward extension to the Victorian enclave of Richmond Terrace and Minto Place remain among the very pleasantest parts of the city in which to live.

Magdalen Yard has seen some stirring events, such as the 'Mass Meeting of the Inhabitants of Dundee on 10th November 1819 at Twelve o'clock noon to consider the present STATE of the COUNTRY, with a view to suggest the means most likely to lead to a REFORM of ABUSES and an alleviation of the distress with which the working classes in particular are nearly overwhelmed'. This upsurge in radical feeling was a direct result of the Peterloo Massacre in Manchester, and produced a crowd of ten thousand people who were addressed by the local politician George **Kinloch** and who listened to his impassioned advocacy of 'one man one vote'. Kinloch was arrested and charged with sedition, but fled into exile before sentence could be passed; he was subsequently pardoned, elected as Dundee's first Reformed Member of Parliament and eventually earned a statue in Albert Square. Sixty-five years after Peterloo the citizenry again assembled at Magdalen Green (as it came to be called) to demonstrate against the Lords' rejection of Gladstone's bill to reform the electoral system.

Many native Dundonians of the older generation had a grandparent who could recall visiting Magdalen Green on the morning of 29 December 1889 to view the ruin of the high girders of the first Tay bridge which had collapsed in a fearsome storm the previous night. But nowadays peace reigns at Magdalen Green, and although cricket and golf practice are *streng verboten* and the tennis courts have gone and the once popular bowling club disbanded, the local populace still frequent 'the Maggie' for sunshine and scenery.

Mains

The term 'Mains', familiar in farm names, is cognate with the words domain, demesne, and originally the Latin *dominium* meaning 'estate'; in practical usage it meant the land farmed by the proprietor himself rather than by tenants, and later simply came to mean the home farm. Such is the origin of the old parish of Mains, united at the beginning of the century to form the parish of Mains and Strathmartine. One is tempted to ask—'Mains of what?', because in normal usage the term is followed by the name of the estate, a point illustrated by the nearby Mains of Baldovan and Mains of Auchterhouse. To the average Dundonian however, the name Mains will be associated with Mains Castle, Den o' Mains and Mill o' Mains.

The name Mains must have been of some importance, for there are no fewer than three Dundee streets which contain it. Mains Loan was the lane which led from the city to the open fields over which a track took the way-farer to the Mains parish and castle; the adjacent Mains Terrace would, at a later period, have been named after the Loan. Mains Road is problematical, for it appears to have led to Trottick Mains rather than to Mains parish. Unnecessary confusion was caused by the naming of Main Street which runs at right angles to Mains Road, but which probably has no etymologi-cal connection with it or with the parish.

Mains is a relatively new name for the castle (see **Fintry**), and the cir-cumstances of the change in nomenclature are unclear. But the history of the castle itself is well established. Built by the Graham family of Fintry over a long period beginning in 1480, it is set on a high bank above the Gelly burn in the Dighty valley. The keystone above the main gate has the initials of David Graham and his wife Dame Margaret Ogilvy, dated 1562, and signalises the perfect realisation of this fine example of a courtyard castle. Sir David Graham was executed thirty years later for his complicity in a plot to re-establish the Catholic religion in Scotland, and the castle's best days were over. It underwent unsuitable alteration and clumsy renova-tion, until around 1740, when it ceased to be inhabited as a dwelling; the whole property was then sold to the Erskines, another old Angus family. They in turn abandoned it when they built their new mansion of **Linlathen**. In 1912 Sir James Caird bought the now ruinous castle along with its exten-sive park and from the latter created the recreation ground known as Caird Park. The castle buildings were acquired by the city in the 1920s but suf-fered further depredation at the hands of local vandals, and the position looked hopeless until restoration began some ten years ago. Mains Castle now functions as an elegant restaurant and has become another jewel in Dundee's crown.

When we see a bus bearing the destination 'Mill o' Mains' (one of the city's newest and most far-flung suburbs) we are reminded of some of the ancient history of Dundee's hinterland. The old mill lay to the east of the Castle, and is known to have existed as early as 1425, although the only visible remains are from the seventeenth century. The nearby white-harled building of 1726 was apparently the tacksman's cottage. The new mill operated as a corn mill from the early 1800s, but in 1948 the water-wheel and the machinery were scrapped—the loss of another potential tourist attraction.

Maryfield

With the disappearance of the tramway system in the 1960s, many of Dundee's more familiar place-names seemed to lose any precise location. Where for example is Downfield, where exactly is **Blackness**? Another prime example is Maryfield, once the location of the terminus for one of the city's busiest routes and a depot for the tramcars themselves. As a district name Maryfield does not appear on the Streetfinder map, and reference to the Dundee Street Directory would give only Maryfield Road in Broughty Ferry (singularly unhelpful) and Maryfield Terrace, a short and insignificant little street connecting Mains Loan and Forfar Road. The area traditionally known as Maryfield in fact is bounded by the Morgan Academy on the south, by Mains Loan on the west, by the Kingsway on the north, and by Pitkerro Road on the east. It tends however to merge with Stobswell on the south; it is the area of the former tram terminus and the late-Victorian houses at the top of the hill that comes to mind when the name is mentioned.

It is sometimes maintained that the Mary in the name refers to the Virgin, who as St Mary was patron saint of the city in succession to St Clement. But the proximity of Janefield suggests rather that the reference is to a Mary of more recent and local fame —possibly the wife or daughter of one of the estate or mill-owners. Maryfield began in the early 1830s as a ribbon-development along the turnpike road to Forfar; side streets sprouted towards Mains Loan on the west and Pitkerro Road on the east, until by the 1870s most of the gaps had been filled and the area had achieved gentility, with the terraced and semi-detached villas of Argyle Street and Lammerton Terrace forming a suburban settlement where resided doctors, solicitors, teachers and other representatives of Dundee's emergent middle-class.

Further down the scale and down the hill was Maryfield Hospital, formerly known as the Eastern Hospital and opened in 1893 'for the treatment of the sick poor under the charge of the Parish Council'. The hospital indeed at one time incorporated a poor-house, a separate and rather distinguished-looking building which however was known by the unattractive name of 'the Grubber'; this place was dreaded by some of the older and more indigent citizenry as being possibly their ultimate abode on this planet. It is fair to add that Maryfield Hospital, when it was brought under the aegis of the NHS in 1948, lost its patronising association with deserving poverty and developed into a first-class general hospital with medical, surgical and obstetric units. When its facilities were transferred to Ninewells in the early 1970s the local community felt a genuine sense of loss.

The whole hospital site has been flattened to provide a recreation ground for Dundee College of Further Education, apart from one building that remains at the north end of the old hospital precinct. This is the former maternity wing of the hospital, and is now the office of the city analyst. This part of Maryfield would be unrecognizable to the returning exile; but the rest of the suburb has changed remarkably little in the past half century.

The Meadows

Meadow is a term that we tend to associate with the gentler scenery of England; indeed in Scotland as well as meaning cultivated pasture it can indicate marshy ground where the rough grass was cut for hay. This appears to be the sense of Edinburgh's Meadows, once the site of a loch; and the same is true in Dundee where 'the Meadows' referred to a marshy area stretching from the present Albert Square almost to Lochee Road. At a very early period three streamlets were dammed to provide power for the Castle mill (see **Castle**), and when these were later culverted the mill dam was removed and the vacant land given 'to the Inhabetants of the Town to serve them for a green to Bleach & cleanse their cloaths upon'; the stream serving this bleachfield was the Scourin Burn, known as the Castle Burn at the point where it ran east of the castle rock.

The south-eastern part, known as the Little Meadow, remained very marshy, and the stagnant pools became a health hazard to the inhabitants of the fashionable eighteenth century Murraygate. The swamp caused great difficulties to the contractors when Reform Street was created in the nineteenth century; even more serious was the subsidence which occurred during the construction of the Royal Exchange in 1854, when plans for the addition of an ornate tower were forcibly abandoned because of the sinking foundations. The whole structure had to be shored up, and the street level lowered in order to accommodate the movement that had taken place in the building.

Meadow Entry and Meadow Place are still to be found on the Dundee map, but more familiar is Meadowside, which was originally named Meadow Street—nicknamed 'Quality Street', for this was an exclusive part of the town. ('Meadowside' was the name of a now-vanished street later covered by Albert Square). The present Meadowside is dominated by the red-stone Courier Building of 1902; it also houses the Post Office building. Meadowside also appears to have been in common parlance the name of the Public Bleaching Green, which was in use until 1825, when the Town Council swapped it for a piece of land in Constitution Road. In more recent memory, the term 'The Meadows' was used for the public wash-houses which stood at the foot of that road.

To the north of the Meadows was an area which appears on old maps as having the curious name of East Chaple Shed. The Scots word 'shed' meant to separate, as it might be the sheep from the goats, and a shed was (and is) a parting in the hair. In place-names it usually becomes shade; and the name is represented now by Chapelshade—that is to say, the division of land pertaining to the chapel (of which nothing is known). Chapel Street leads from Meadowside to New Inn Entry. Chapelshade doesn't appear on the map but formed part of the name of Rosebank church; East Chapelshade had been sold to the Town Council, and early in the last century became a built-up area containing two horseshoe layouts of high-class residential building; West Chapelshade remained under cultivation for somewhat longer but was eventually subject to unplanned industrial development.

To the south of West Chapelshade was 'the **Ward**', another dialect term meaning an enclosed meadowland (see **Magdalen Yard**); in modern usage 'ward' is a municipal division. Ward Road was opened in 1803, and the whole area was to be covered with buildings (mainly non-residential) in the next half century; one of these was a 'school of industry', an early euphemism for an establishment for juvenile delinquents, and although the boys were later transferred elsewhere (in the worst cases to the *Mars* training ship) the errant girls remained at Ward Road until the end of the century.

Menzieshill

Before the 1960s not many people in Dundee had heard of the name Menzieshill. This is hardly surprising, for it was merely an eminence over-looking the old Perth Road at Ninewells. There was a farm of the name on the Invergowrie estate, reachable by a track leading from Greystane House (now the Swallow Hotel) to the Balgay Cemetery. This terrain, which in living memory was rolling meadowland, is now entirely covered by the Kingsway, by the Dundee Technology Park, by Ninewells Hospital—and of course by the new suburb of Menzieshill.

As you approach Dundee on the A90 from Perth your first sight of the city is stunning. Menzieshill, which dominates the scene, makes Dundee look like a metropolis of the future. So it is, possibly; and Menzieshill is an example which deserves to be followed—a true suburb, with a High School, two primary schools, a church, a police station, a post-office—and a bird's eye view of one of the best hospitals in Europe. Menzieshill was built between 1960 and 1965 as part of the process of clearing some of the remaining overcrowded areas nearer to the centre of the city; and if its five fifteen-storey blocks of flats are not perhaps to everybody's taste, at least an attempt has been made to preserve the balance between high-density housing on the one hand and spacious living on the other.

An odd thing about Menzieshill is that it has a pre-history and a future, but no recent history to speak of. Stone coffins were found here, evidence of human settlement in the Dundee area from prehistoric times (dating from as early as 6000 BC); and indeed the situation is so favourable that it is something of a miracle that it was not developed during the mediaeval or early modern periods. But nobody now remembers who the Menzies was who gave his name to the farm or to the hill; at a guess, he may have flourished around the end of the eighteenth century. Prior to that Menzieshill does not figure in the records.

Menzies has been a familiar Perthshire surname from mediaeval times; originally from the Norman name Mesnières (which is related to the noun demesne, a manor), it came to this country through the English surname Manners. We have cause to rejoice, however, that Menzieshill is invariably (and correctly) pronounced 'Mingiz-hill' by Dundonians. If only this pronunciation were to be applied to other occurrences of the name—stationers, former Australian prime ministers and the like—a deal of unnecessary irritation would be avoided to those of us who dislike the sound 'Menzaze'.

Monifieth

The name is usually taken to be from the Gaelic *moine feith*—'bog marsh'; and although Monifeith is noted for its dry sandy links you have to remember that the name originally referred to a largish parish, stretching from the eastern boundary of Dundee to Barry, and taking in the hinterland almost to Monikie. Moreover, the parish contains a burn known as the Fithie, almost certainly the same word as *feith*. The old parish comprised the villages of Barnhill and most of Broughty Ferry, with the present Monifieth at its eastern extremity; at the end of the eighteenth century the village consisted of not more than sixty houses, mostly thatched and straggling along the north side of its single street.

Monifieth is known to have been the site of a Culdee monastic community. Since this term is widely used but little understood, it may be worth mentioning that the *Cele de* ('vassals of God') were a reformist offshoot of the Celtic church who established themselves in various parts of eastern Scotland in the ninth century, including St Andrews, Abernethy and Brechin.

102

No Culdee traces remain in Monifieth, however, and we have to skip a few centuries to understand the development of the village from a kirktoun to a sizeable suburb (see **Kirkton**).

The coastland is low and sandy, ill-adapted for natural anchorages, and Monifieth was never a maritime or fishing settlement. Rather it owes its existence to the fertility of the soil to the north, and was in the nature of an agricultural centre; as late as 1800 a twice-yearly market for cattle and horses was held in the village, whose inhabitants were mainly employed on the land. Others were hand-loom weavers who supplied material for the Dundee manufactories.

The Dighty water, descending from the raised beaches above Panmure to enter the sea at Monifieth, generated enough power to drive a large spinning mill. But Monifieth never became industrial, as did many Angus villages, and the iron foundry at the Milton was initially for the manufacture of carts and ploughs. Later in the nineteenth century it became an engineering works making textile machinery.

Despite the dismissive statement in an old guide book that 'there is nothing much at Monifieth to tempt you to linger', it must in fact have been a pleasant spot, with its rolling hills to the north, the long line of the Buddon links to the east and the view up-river to the west. But as happened in the case of **Broughty**, the railway severed the village from the beach; and the introduction in 1905 of a tramway from Dundee led to large-scale commuter-type development. This latter was not bad in itself, and Monifieth has whole streets of pleasant south-facing Edwardian villas (each with its blind over the front door to prevent the sun from blistering the paint). From the 1950s onwards the village grew massively on its outskirts, without any corresponding improvement in the centre; in this respect it resembles Barnhill more than it does Broughty Ferry, a suburb of much greater character. However, although Monifieth was officially re-absorbed into the County of Angus in the boundary revision of 1996, these suburbs are now for practical purposes part of the greater Dundee and have lost much of their former distinction.

The recent history of Monifieth illustrates one of the difficulties of modern urban planning. The vast and rapid expansion of the village consisted largely of suburban housing for first-time buyers; these were mainly young-marrieds, attracted to Dundee by jobs in high technology industry and in higher education, and in the nature of things there duly occurred something of an explosion in the infant population. Additional primary schooling had to be built, some of which must in course of time have become superfluous when the first cohort of pupils had passed through the system. Perhaps not a serious problem, for modern Monifieth is still a good place to live, and no doubt the supply of children has been or will be renewed.

Morgan

Names of Dundee's older institutions are almost invariably preceded by the definite article—*the* Hawkhill, *the* Caird Hall, *the* DRI. Thus, Morgan Academy is always known as 'The Morgan' and similar treatment is given to the names of its rivals 'The Harris' and 'The High'. But not much thought is given nowadays to the man who gave his name to the Morgan Academy.

John Morgan was a self-made millionaire, of rather unappealing character, who turned in his last years to large-scale philanthropy. His vast wealth had given him ideas of grandeur which he strove to reinforce by tracing an imaginary descent from Norman-French nobility, and he produced some rather fanciful etymologies of his surname. In fact, Morgan is a reasonably frequent name in Scotland (although commoner in England and Wales) and there have been Morgans in Angus since the thirteenth century. John Morgan's grandfather was a tenant farmer near Forfar and his father was a Dundee tavern-keeper in Kirk Wynd near the old Overgate. John was born in 1766, and his brother Thomas four years later (there were also other siblings). John was destined for the law, Thomas for medicine; both joined the East India Company and went to Calcutta, John as a 'free merchant' and Thomas as a doctor. Both made hefty fortunes up country, and in 1812 after an absence of 28 years they returned to Dundee.

Morgan *père* had meantime died in abject poverty, and the two Morgan brothers took over the mansion of Balgay, where they set up house for themselves and for the four remaining members of the family. But the local citizenry, as often happened in Dundee, did not accept the nabob status of the incomers ('Eh kent ees faither') and the entire family in resentment migrated to Haddington in 1815. None of them married, and they later set up house in a fashionable part of Edinburgh, where one by one they eventually died.

John Morgan had long had in mind the establishment in Dundee of an institution on the lines of George Heriot's Hospital, and prepared plans for a boarding-school for 650 boys, 'the sons of tradesmen and persons of the working-class generally whose parents stand in need of assistance'. The education was to be monastic in character, and pupils were to be spared the 'more degrading kinds of corporal punishment'. Unfortunately Morgan became senile in his last years, and made frequent and unclear alterations to his will. On his death in 1850 his executors were faced with three sets of conflicting instructions, which could be resolved only by resort to the Court of Session, and ultimately to the House of Lords. The costs of all this resulted

104

in a considerable diminution in the amount of the capital, and there was a huge delay in the realisation of Morgan's plans for the hospital. The building was however begun in 1863 and completed five years later, although with considerably fewer pupils than Morgan had originally envisaged. It functioned for less than twenty years as a 'hospital' (boarding school) and was then sold to the Dundee School Board as a secondary day-school. Morgan Academy, as it came to be officially called, lost its working- class aura and developed into a fully comprehensive school of some academic distinction.

John Morgan was a true benefactor to his native city, if not quite in the way that he intended. Dundee in turn appreciated his generosity, but not to the extent of following his trustees' explicit instructions for the upkeep of the family tomb in the Howff.

Murraygate

The names Murray and Moray are essentially the same, with the meaning of 'sea settlement'. It was not until the eighteenth century that the convention was adopted of having Moray as a place-name and Murray as a surname. Murraygate is thought to have been named by or after Randolph, earl of Moray, the companion-in-arms of Wallace and Bruce: so the name probably means 'Moray's street', and if this is correct the street would date from the early fourteenth century.

In fact the thoroughfare is probably older, since it formed the principal means of egress from the castle (see **Castle**) to the north-east. It has undergone vast changes before becoming what is arguably now the principal shopping street in Dundee, and certainly the most attractive. Nothing remains to suggest its mediaeval appearance, but in the late eighteenth century it is described as 'very broad' and 'almost new built from end to end, with Stately Stone buildings that make goodly Appearance'. These were the residences of the gentry, who hibernated in town and returned to their country estates with the arrival of the better weather (the reverse of what was happening in such places as Bath and London, where the fashionable season to be in town was spring and early summer). At least one of these houses of 'goodly Appearance' is still to be seen (on the north-west side, above the pend of Meadow Entry); and the term 'very broad' must have referred only to the western end, for the other part was known as 'the Narrow'. The name Meadow Entry, which led to the open fields (see **Meadows**) is a reminder of the semi-rural state of the central parts of the town. (Panmure Street was created at a later date to provide better access to the Meadows.)

The Murraygate that we now know dates mainly from a further rebuilding in the 1860s, which eliminated the narrows and provided the street with such fine buildings as the classical Bank of Scotland. Later building was more varied in style, but who can forget the art deco cinema called La Scala ('*the* La Scala' in Dundee parlance) or the inimitable house-style of Woolworths (now the home of Tesco Metro). And of course the whole area was transformed by the pedestrianisation which took place in the 1970s, with the tramlines still *in situ* and attractive lamp standards down the centre, all showing what can be done by a process of tasteful conservation.

The closing of the **Wellgate** and the erection of the Wellgate Centre have altered the old prospect to the north (up the Wellgate steps and on through the **Hilltown**), and the Murraygate now ends rather abruptly at the junction of Panmure Street and the Cowgate. The latter was the lane by which the cattle were taken out through the Port (see **Wishart**) to the pasture beyond; but the Cowgate was soon to lose its bovine associations, and, surrounded by mills and factories, became the quarter of Dundee's linen trade, the city's most important industry until the arrival of jute in the nineteenth century. St Andrews Square (where it adjoined King Street) was a favourite meeting-place for the merchants and traders. The finest feature of this area is St Andrews Church, a simple but impressive building of the 1770s (see under **Bell**).

The Cowgate is now curtailed by the inner ring road, and consequently one of the shortest streets in Dundee; it has nothing much to say for itself other than a nameless Edwardian structure in red sandstone. Built as the King's Theatre, its days of glory lasted barely twenty years before it became the Gaumont Cinema in 1928. It was lately given over to County Bingo (surely a contradiction in terms?) and is now derelict and defaced. One can only hope that the conservationists' plans for restoring this ill-treated building may be successfully realised.

Newport

As the name implies, this settlement owes its existence to the need for ferry services across the Tay. There were at one time several of these, stretching for ten miles along the river; they are known to have existed in the reign of William the Lion in the eleventh century. The right to run ferries originally pertained to the various estates on which the terminals were situated— from east to west these were Port-on-Craig (see **Tayport**), Sea Mylnes (belonging to the Naughton estate), Woodhaven (belonging to the Sandford estate) and Balmerino (belonging to the Abbey).

In the late sixteenth century Henry Kynnaird of that Ilk became commendator of Balmerino Abbey and owner of the Sea Mylnes ('sea mills') at what is now Newport. In 1595 his son Patrick was granted by the Privy

Council the lucrative monopoly of ferry crossings of the Tay. This right was not unnaturally opposed by the burgesses of Dundee, and there began a long and acrimonious dispute between the two parties on either side of the river. The plague intervened, and the town council secured a temporary victory by banning ferry traffic of any kind. Patrick Kinnaird's charter was however confirmed by Parliament, with permission for ferry passengers to land unmolested 'at the Craigs of Dundee' (later to be known as the Craig Pier, and now Discovery Point). The story ends in anti-climax, for the privileges of the Kinnairds eventually lapsed and the Tay Ferries became a municipal concern which lasted for almost over 350 years—in fact, until the road bridge opened in 1967.

Early in the eighteenth century the need had become obvious for more extensive facilities for the ferries on the south side of the river; and so the Dundee authorities acquired land from the estates of Sandford and Inverdovat (now Tayfield) to construct a new harbour with pier and granaries and to develop the hamlet of Sea Mylnes. The new village was to be called 'New Port of Dundee' but it was apparently known at various times as New Dundee and South Port. In common usage it became Newport—not perhaps a terribly imaginative name, and one which occurs at least ten times in various parts of England and Wales: 'Newport-on-Tay' was a name devised by the Post Office to avoid confusion,

To begin with, the village amenities at Newport consisted of little more than the ferry terminal, with a corn mill and a salmon fishing station; but the construction of a new turnpike road from Cupar allowed Newport to develop in importance. In 1841 its population was a mere 260; it must now be more than twenty times that number. The Woodhaven ferry, conveniently linked with the rest of Fife by the old turnpike road which crossed the hills at the Wormit gap, had at one time been widely used. But the increasing size of the Middle Bank (a sandbank in the middle of the river north of Woodhaven) made the Newport crossing more reliable, and the Woodhaven ferry finally folded in 1822. Thereafter Newport became the principal non-industrial settlement south of the river. With the opening of the railway bridge in 1870 Newport grew into a dormitory suburb and (perhaps surprisingly) a holiday resort. But for the best part of a century the ferries continued to flourish, and the 'Fifie' crossing to Newport, followed by a stroll along the braes, was long a favourite outing for Dundonians.

Newport is therefore quite an ancient port, and a somewhat older village than Wormit with which it is now continuous. (Wormit, shown on the 1827 map as a farm, became a railway village with the establishment in 1891 of a North British Railway Company station on the line to Tayport.) The configuration of the landscape, with a line of hills rising steeply from the shore, has confined building to a fairly narrow strip; even with the coming of the road bridge, which greatly increased the potential for commuting, Newport and Wormit have remained pleasantly residential and small-sized suburbs. The name of the latter has caused some mystification: it probably comes from the personal name Orme, who was the original recipient of a charter of lands in Balmerino Parish from William the Lion. There is apparently no intended reference to serpents or worms.

Ninewells

Ninewells was a farm on the old road between Dundee and Invergowrie. Between the 1930s and the 1960s it achieved much greater celebrity as the name of a tramway terminus on the extreme western boundary of the city, where for the expenditure of threepence or so you could on a summer's evening enjoy one of the finest pieces of river scenery in Britain. Now the name is internationally known as that of a prestigious hospital, a description of whose state-of-the-art magnificence would be outside the compass of the present volume.

But a subtle change has crept into the pronunciation of the name: it used to be Nine*wells*, the name being supposedly based on a half-forgotten legend of the existence of water sources to that number in the vicinity (one of them reputedly in the garden of Fernbrae Hospital); and the important word was *wells*. But nowadays you are just as likely to hear the pronunciation *Nine*wells, as if to distinguish it from a hypothetical place with eight wells or ten wells. This soundshift provides a good illustration of the southern tendency to stress the first syllable of a name (*Lon*don, *Bir*mingham) whereas Scots and Gaelic often put the stress elsewhere according to the meaning. The tendency is annoying when it creeps into the rendering of such Scottish names as *Avie*more and *Mont*rose; and intolerable in the American pronunciation of Inverness which is made to scan like 'wilderness' and makes nonsense of the etymology. As it happens, however, recent scholarship has suggested a derivation of the prefix of the name Ninewells from St Ninian who, let us pretend to remember, was a fifth-century Christian bishop responsible for carrying the gospel to the Picts south of the Grampians. The cult of Ninian was revived in the twelfth century, and his name and ministry are widely commemorated. There are several places called Ninewells in eastern Scotland, one of them in North Fife. If the Ninianic derivation is indeed correct, the stress would be on the first syllable of the place-name; so it may well be that the new pronunciation of *Nine*wells is in fact correct, and preferable to the old one.

Ninewells hospital with its sunny and airy rooms, broad corridors and splendid patient facilities is an excellent place to be if one is ill, and the staff seem to be equally appreciative of the working conditions. But nowhere more than in Ninewells can one observe the difference between the old Dundee and the new. You can still hear the homely Dundee voices—but with decreasing frequency, compared with the old days of Maryfield and DRI. Partly this is because the surroundings are more inhibiting, the personnel more cosmopolitan: a Dundee wifie from the old Hilltown would have had difficulty in making herself understood in conversation with a Chinese houseman or a Pakistani nurse, but her grandchildren successfully make the effort. More important is the fact that Broad Scots in any of its varieties is in retreat because the world it described is no longer with us. Scots (and Gaelic) have largely lost the ability to coin new words: there is no Scots dialect word for gastroscopy, nor for that matter a Gaelic word for chemotherapy. Conversely there are no English equivalents for Scots terms such as *stathels* (the mushroom-shaped stones used as the base for constructing a corn-stack) or for *boorach* (a mixed-up pile) because corn-stacks are obsolete and black bin-bags have taken the place of refuse heaps. An attempt to revive the old language would have to be accompanied by a return from a technological to an agrarian society—a hopeless enterprise if ever there was one.

That does not lessen one's regret at the passing of the old ways; indeed it makes one cherish the memory of them. And you will still at Ninewells get flashes of the old Dundee tongue from the less august personnel. Like the porter pushing the trolley bearing an ill and apprehensive patient to theatre and remarking to the cleaner polishing the floor—'Ye're makkin a brah joab o't'. To which she replied 'Eh. See yer fiss in it, aye!' The patient was greatly comforted by this piece of normal conversation and duly survived to write the little book which is now in your hands.

Orchar

The first thing to be said about this name is that it is a variant of Urquhart and has nothing to do with orchards. This caution would have been unnecessary a century ago, when the name was frequently pronounced: now it is more usually to be seen in print. The second thing is that it is nowadays current mainly in Broughty Ferry, although its fame in Dundee was at one time almost as great.

James Guthrie Orchar was born in 1825 on the estate of **Craigie** near the present Pitkerro Road, the son of a joiner and cartwright. James's was the typical Victorian success story: with only an elementary schooling, he was apprenticed to his father as a joiner, but soon became interested in engineering. He got a job in the old Wallace Foundry (see **Wallace**), which had the contract for building the locomotives for the Dundee and Perth Railway. After a spell in England he went into partnership in Dundee with William Robertson and took over the Wallace Foundry; the partners concentrated on the manufacture of machinery for spinning and weaving flax and jute, at which they were spectacularly successful. When the needs of the Dundee mills had been satisfied, Robertson and Orchar began to extend the firm's services to the newly-established jute mills in Calcutta; this allowed the Indians to process jute for themselves and may in the long run have contributed to the downfall of jute in Dundee—but not before both William Robertson and James Orchar had made their fortunes.

Both men combined their great wealth with respectability and good works. Orchar took a prominent part in the affairs of the community, and in 1886 was elected Provost of Broughty Ferry (which was of course a separate municipality until 1913). He held that position for twelve years, and apparently enjoyed great popularity. This is hardly surprising, for his benefactions include Orchar Park (on the south side of Monifieth Road) and the landscaping of Reres Hill; but he was also reputed to be a very genial and sociable man and a gifted raconteur.

It is particularly as an art collector and patron of music that Orchar deserves to be remembered. From the 1860s he began to collect paintings and musical instruments, about all of which he was knowledgeable. Dundee at that time was very art-conscious, and Orchar was instrumental in arranging a series of annual exhibitions (for which he lent many of his own paintings). Under his will he left his entire collection to a trust for the benefit of the public of Broughty Ferry; he had intended that it should be housed in a new building to be erected at Reres Hill, but in the event the endowment funds were used to acquire instead the villa at number 31 Beach Crescent (which, incidentally, had been the family home of the Stephens, builders of the *Discovery*). It was this house which was to become the Orchar Gallery; and only the commemorative Jubilee Arch at Reres Hill is there to remind Broughty of Orchar's intentions.

Orchar died in 1898, and the Gallery survived him by less than a century. In 1979 a shortage of recurrent funding left the Trustees with no alternative but to close the Gallery and entrust the contents to Dundee Galleries and Museums (who have proved to be worthy curators of these paintings, some of which are of great beauty). This move was unwelcome to the Ferry folk, but it was no doubt inevitable, for Orchar's collection was of contemporary (i.e. Victorian) painting, which by the mid-twentieth century had only a limited appeal. There were no funds for adding to the collection or extending its scope; and the result would probably have been no different had the projected building at Reres Hill materialised. So 31 Beach Crescent is now the Orchar Nursing Home—still a benefit to Broughty Ferry, but hardly in the way that Orchar had intended.

Overgate

The Overgate (formerly spelt Overgait, and meaning 'the upper street') was one of the oldest thoroughfares in the city, and is still held in great affection in the memories of older Dundonians. It ran from the foot of Reform Street to the West Port (which was on the site of the similarly-named modern traffic roundabout). An earlier name for Overgait was Argylesgait, probably because the Campbells of Balruddery had a town house there, in what was then a rather posh area of the mediaeval burgh; but it is possibly of earlier origin, dating from the time of a Gaelic-speaking settlement (the name Argyle was originally *Oirer Ghaidheal*—'district of the Gael'). Until the eighteenth century the Overgate was a pleasant semi-rural place, referred to by an anonymous contemporary writer as 'Overgate Gardens' and separated by a fine hedge from the **Ward**.

The Overgate was never an imposing street, but it was rich in history and atmosphere, having remained untouched by the provisions of the Improvement Acts of the 1870s (unlike other 'gaits' such as Murraygate and Seagate, which had been widened and reconstructed). The 1850 gazetteer describes the lower reaches of the Overgate in these terms: 'At the west end of High-street, closing up the area, is an ancient building, long called the Luckenbooths ['lockable shops'], on the corner of which is still a turret indicative of its former character. This venerable pile was the adopted residence of General Monck, when he entered Dundee and consigned it to the pillage of his soldiery; and it was the birthplace of the celebrated Anne Scott, daughter of the Earl of Buccleuch and afterwards Duchess of Monmouth, whose parents had sought refuge in the town from the effects of Cromwell's usurpation'. The gazetteer further says that 'it was also, in 1715, the adopted home of the Pretender during the period of his stay in Dundee', but a competing claim that he lodged at Castle Hill House (see **Castle Street**) is now more widely believed. The English poet and humorist Thomas Hood spent part of his youth in the town, and made his literary debut in the *Dundee Advertiser*; there used to be an inscribed plate on the north side of Overgate at this spot to mark the house where he stayed.

The decline came in the mid-Victorian era when the street was colonised by spinners and weavers, the properties divided and workshops set up in the former gardens or 'backlands'. But even so, the street never quite lost its character and was rather charming in its own repulsive way. One remembers the old-fashioned 'shoppies', entered down stone steps and indicative of the mediaeval street-level; a bell pinged on entry and Miss Quaid would serve boilings in a twist of paper. And the prodigious number of pubs, sufficient to satisfy the drouth of the whole city; and the crunch of whelk-shells underfoot on a Saturday night. And the noise and the smells…

But enough of nostalgia: this was the Overgate of yesteryear, ruthlessly swept away in the 1960s to make way for the Overgate Shopping Centre, whose east end is just tolerable but which westwards degenerates into something resembling a run-down South American city. The old cobbled Overgate is no more, and the little concrete canyon of a lane that now bears its name is just a horrid mockery. Gone also are the fascinating little streets and alleys that bisected it: Tally Street, which was a southern continuation of Barrack Street, and boasting once-fashionable shops and even a hotel; Thorter Row (really 'thwart' or 'cross' row or lane), a paved and bustling alleyway of surprisingly little length; and by contrast Long Wynd, the site of a week-end market and containing a fragment of the city wall.

It is undeniable that the old Overgate, congested from the early nineteenth century onwards, had become a slum with a reputation for prostitution, drunkenness and every sort of crime ranging from petty theft to murder. Most of its inhabitants, one imagines, were glad to see it go. It was however neither the narrowness of the thoroughfare nor the disorderliness of its inhabitants which sealed the fate of this little old street: it was the fact that Dundee's local sandstone was liable to turn a dirty brown with age and to crumble and lose all architectural detail. Very few Dundee buildings made from this stone survive—but look at the line of decrepit warehouses running south from the timber yard near the *Unicorn* and you will get a reminder of how sad the Overgate would now appear. (By contrast, other properties such as Camperdown House, the High School and David Winters' which were built of expensive imported stone have kept their fine appearance).

Despite all this, something might nevertheless have been saved, and one has only to look at the Shambles in York to see the extent of Dundee's loss; but bear in mind that in the 1950s 'progress' was everything and the word 'conservation' was barely in the dictionary let alone in the vocabulary of officialdom. Of the Overgate there is now nothing left to conserve, but the long-rumoured reconstruction of the shopping centre appears to be imminent, and already the Thistle Hotel has closed its doors. Whatever replaces these poverty-stricken and misconceived buildings can hardly fail to be an improvement.

Panmure

An interesting name, which seems to be purely Pictish in origin and therefore earlier than most of the Gaelic nomenclature of Angus. It is thought to come from the words *pant mawr* meaning 'large hollow' and is the name of an estate to the north of Monifieth. As might have been expected, the name has been borrowed for several streets in Monifieth and Broughty Ferry — six of them if you include the new Panmurefield Road and Terrace near Monifieth High School. Dundee also has its Panmure Street and Terrace, both named after a particular nobleman who was one of the city's benefactors; and the name has also gained currency as that of a Rugby Football club, a Golf Club and at least two hotels.

To go back to the beginning, in the eleventh century William the Lion, King of Scots, granted the lands of Benvie to Philip Valones, descendant of a Norman grandee, as a reward for services in connection with the king's release from captivity in England. A Valones heiress married into the Maule family, who had come into the possession of the estate of Panmure; these properties were to remain with the Maules for twenty generations until they were forfeited after the Jacobite Rising of 1715, earl James of Panmure having fallen at the battle of Sheriffmuir. Thereafter the property passed to the earls of Dalhousie, one of whom took the name of Maule. The Panmure title was eventually restored in the reign of George IV.

Meanwhile there had appeared on the statute book the Improvements Bill of 1824, designed to alleviate downtown slum conditions. Dundee Town Council resolved to drive a new street through some decaying property in order to connect the Cowgate with the Meadows; the necessary demolitions were carried out and the thoroughfare opened in 1839. It was agreed to name the new street after William Ramsay Maule, first Baron Panmure, in recognition of 'his recent munificent donations to the funds of the Infirmary' (see **DRI**). Panmure Terrace to the north of Dudhope was named with the same motive.

The Infirmary was not Lord Panmure's only good turn to Dundee: in 1847 he parted with some of his lands to allow the formation of the Monikie and Crombie reservoirs. This was an attempt to overcome Dundee's perennial water problems, and for a time it was successful. The water was piped to the **Stobsmuir** reservoir in the city, and distributed throughout the town— a great improvement on the previous arrangement (see under **Wellgate**), and one which served the city until the development of Lintrathen in 1874.

It seems that the 1st Baron ranked high in domestic as well as public esteem. On a hill to the north of the Arbroath Road there is a prominent landmark known as the Panmure monument. No mere obelisk, it is more than a hundred feet high with a spiral staircase leading to a balcony, and was 'raised by subscription amongst the tenants of the Panmure estate as a testimonial to Lord Panmure' in 1839.

Pitkerro

In the sixteenth century the laird of Pitkerro was one James Durham, and it is on record that he complained to Mary, Queen of Scots that he had been obliged to flee his own house 'in fear and danger of his life'. This was on account of the vicious and unreasonable behaviour of his nearest neighbour, Henry Lovell of **Ballumbie**; and it must have been doubly vexatious, for it was only recently (1554) that Durham had built a new mansion at Pitkerro. Durham was described by a contemporary as 'ane sober and poor gentleman' (then as now, 'poor' must have been a relative term). There is a tradition, unverified but not unlikely, that in 1562 Mary, Queen of Scots stayed at Pitkerro on her journey north to quell Huntly's rebellion. Thereafter, although the estate did not long remain in the hands of any one family, a nineteenth-century account describes the mansion as being 'in the castellated manner, with the burn of Murroes wimpling along the north side of the grounds'. Pitkerro is still a very lovely place; and there is a temptation to compare it with the sad dereliction of Ballumbie and to draw the appropriate moral.

In 1904 the house was restored and greatly extended by Sir Robert Lorimer (architect of *inter alia* the Scottish National War Memorial in Edinburgh Castle); occupied by Polish troops during the 1939 war, it became derelict and the grounds overgrown. In the 1950s the property was bought by a group of young people and became home to a small Catholic lay community in the Diocese of Dunkeld; although now subdivided into flats, it preserves its fine external appearance, together with the magnificent gates and lodge at the end of the drive.

For every Dundonian who has admired Pitkerro House, however, there will be a few thousand who have traversed Pitkerro Road. The naming of streets can be an arbitrary business, as explained in the **Introduction**: not so with Pitkerro Road, which more or less chose its own name as being at that time the direct and only way from the town centre to Pitkerro. (But no longer, for Pitkerro Road has been hijacked by the new Longhaugh Road, which would take you in a wrong direction.) The minor oddity remains, that Pitkerro consists of a mansion and a farm and there has never in historical times been a village of the name. But there were in the sixteenth century two mills on the Pitkerro lands, using the Fithie burn as the motive power for corn grinding. These were of some importance and one of them was bought by the city to augment the town mills and rebuilt as late as 1908; it was in operation until comparatively recently. It is possible therefore that this is why the road was named in connection with Pitkerro and not the more important mill downstream at Baldovie which is on the same route, and was the location of a toll-house on the turnpike road to Letham.

The name Pitkerro is instructive in its own right. The *pit* element is discussed in the **Introduction**: 'Pitkerro' is taken to mean 'quarter-share' (and provides a good illustration of the theory which ascribes greater antiquity and importance to *pit* names; it also shows that many Gaelic place-names are functional rather than romantic in origin). Pitkerro's situation is advantageous and its soil has always been fertile, in contrast to areas such as nearby Balmossie which was rough moorland until the 1750s. The inference must be that nearby Ballumbie was less favourably situated than Pitkerro, although the agricultural improvements of the late eighteenth century may have remedied this.

Reform

The 1830s in Scotland were marked by a vast constitutional upheaval which saw the end of the eighteenth century system of political management by the ruling aristocracy and patronage by the land-owning classes. The reactionary government of the Duke of Wellington had come to an end in 1830, and for the next century the running of Scotland was to be largely in the hands of middle-class liberals. The watershed was the Reform Act of 1832, deplored as unpatriotic by traditional Tories such as Sir Walter Scott but welcomed by the Scottish populace at large. Indeed the Reform movement caused very much more popular stir than (so far, at least) has the recent legislation setting up a Scottish parliament. This is perhaps surprising, for the 1832 Act fell far short of instituting universal suffrage, and merely enfranchised males of the respectable middle classes. Nevertheless it did enable Dundee for the first time to have its own member of parliament (see **Kinloch**) and to achieve some of the other aims of the recently-formed Dundee Political Union (including a secret ballot).

The Reform movement and the beginning of the Victorian era coincided with a surge in public building and urban expansion, and many a Scottish burgh renamed one of its principal streets to commemorate the passing of the Act: even Kirriemuir has its Reform Street. In Dundee we did things on a larger scale, although it has to be admitted that the name of Reform Street was something of an afterthought. The streets of the mediaeval burgh ran mainly in an east-west direction, and there developed a need for north-south thoroughfares to connect with the harbour and the shore;

Castle Street, Crichton Street and Lower Commercial Street were constructed to fulfil this need, while Reform Street was to provide a link to the north. The opportunity was to be taken to dignify the city with fine buildings, and if the original Regency concept of Reform Street had been realised, of a row of pilastered and balustraded shops with grand office premises above, Dundee would indeed have something to boast about. So great however were the street's construction costs (which included the removal of a hill at the northern end) that the local wags proposed the name Mortgage Place or Bond Street.

Reform Street was for long Dundee's financial centre, but most of the splendid palatial banks have been converted for other purposes (such as high-quality pubs); others have given place to Building Societies, and some of the attractive old shops have been replaced by hideous fly-by-night boutiques which have in turn gone out of business. Pedestrianisation of the southernmost part has been an improvement—but you have to use your imagination to realise the concept of Reform Street as one of Dundee's finest nineteenth-century thoroughfares.

Riddoch

Two hundred years ago the name Riddoch was associated in the Dundee mind with the forces of reaction, authoritarianism and oppression—not to speak of accusations of corruption, which later and for a time became almost a civic tradition in Dundee. But no street or public building was called after Riddoch, and nowadays the name is unknown to all save historians and antiquarians.

Alexander Riddoch was elected Treasurer of the Burgh in 1776 and became Provost a year later. He dominated the affairs of the municipality for over thirty years, and earned a degree of unpopularity rarely seen since then. He was regarded by most townspeople as an outsider (he came from Comrie) and an upstart (he was a highly successful cloth-merchant, turned property entrepreneur); and to his opponents he was an out-and-out scoundrel, accused of all manner of offences including insider dealing and the diversion of public funds into his own pocket. But it has to be said that a House of Commons select committee, set up to investigate various deficiencies in municipal government in Scotland, could not find the alleged malpractices of Riddoch and the other councillors to be proven. The situation in Dundee, the committee found, was no worse than elsewhere in Scotland, where self-perpetuating oligarchies had been the norm since the later middle ages.

The truth is probably that Riddoch was a wily autocrat and a man with his eye ever on the main chance, and lacking the wider vision that could have inspired the creation of a more beautiful inner city. In the early 1800s, the time when Aberdeen was laying out Union Street and King Street, Dundee's building programme was practically zero—a situation from which it never really recovered. Riddoch would probably have argued that he (temporarily) saved the municipality from bankruptcy, and it is also true that he had some positive achievements to his credit. One thinks of such projects as street-widening and improvement (he was responsible for Castle Street, Crichton Street and Union Street) and of the development of the dock area, which, however controversial, was largely his brain-child.

Also to Riddoch's credit, his strong personality allowed him to handle successfully the disorders in 1792, when revolutionary fervour was threatening to spread from France to industrial Scotland; despite severe provocation from the mob who forced him to join in their egalitarian chanting round the Mercat Cross, he managed to persuade the rioters to return home peaceably. He was, it must be added, forming plans (which he later carried out) to end the turmoil with the aid of a detachment of the military from Perth.

Peace having been restored, one likes to imagine that he himself walked the few hundred yards westward to the splendid house specially built for him in the Nethergate. Whether or not designed by Samuel Bell, it remains a perfect example of a late eighteenth-century Dundee town house and deserves to be better known. Perhaps, as Dundee continues on its voyage of re-discovery, 176 Nethergate may one day relinquish or share its commercial function and be opened to the public as a reminder of these stirring times.

Riverside

You don't require an antique map of the Tay estuary to show the vast amount of land that has been reclaimed from the mud in the last two hundred years: a glance at the modern landscape from road or railway will remind you of the former shoreline. Look at the steep rise of the Seabraes, the slope of the Magdalen Green, the cliffs below the University Botanic Garden—and it will be obvious that the landscape to the south of this elevated terrain is completely man-made. The largest stretch of open ground hereabouts is known as Riverside Park, which now contains the University Recreation Ground and Dundee's airport.

As long ago as 1860 the town authorities had resolved on a long-term programme of land-reclamation, which was to start at Craig Pier and progress steadily westward. The ultimate object was to extend the sea wall to Kingoodie, thus eliminating Invergowrie Bay and its mud-flats. The Corporation's aim was not only—or even mainly—to create amenity ground, but also to fill the space within the sea-wall with the city's rubbish—which in those days consisted, among other things, of large amounts of ash and cinders. So it was that the land reclaimed was universally known as 'the Cowp' (*anglice*, the tip), and it was only after the Great War that the more elegant name of Riverside Park was adopted. The park still showed its origins, with a hard cinder surface, and was not grassed over for another fifty years. It was also a convenient repository for industrial waste, of which there was an abundant supply: damp jute is subject to spontaneous combustion, and smouldering piles of the stuff could be seen left lying on the Cowp for a cooling-off period.

Riverside Park was covered mainly by football pitches, but there was sufficient space to hold on two separate occasions the Royal Highland Show (in 1933 and 1948, before it moved to its permanent site at Ingliston). At one time there was also an open-air swimming-pool, just east of the railway footbridge: this may have been attractive when it was constructed, but by the 1930s it was a revolting place with primitive changing-cubicles and unclean sea-water, and it did not survive the 1939 war. In the days before the Olympian Leisure Centre was built one always talked about 'the baths': those at Riverside Park were called 'the Cowpers' to distinguish them from the more up-market 'Shorers' on the harbour wall (in turn demolished as part of the road-bridge landfall).

Between Craig Pier and Riverside Park the reclaimed land was used for the railway line and the marshalling yards, but to the south of the carriageway was the Esplanade: the past tense is not inappropriate, for the Esplanade seems to have fallen on evil days, and is no longer pedestrian-friendly. It is to be hoped that the present arrangements are only temporary: on a summer evening the mile-long river walk from the 'Fifie' terminal along the tree-lined Esplanade to Magdalen Green used to be a delight.

The whole of the harbour area was of course also reclaimed, Dock Street having marked the old shoreline. It was apparently possible at one time to walk the five miles from Ninewells to Stannergate along something akin to an esplanade: nowadays one would have to negotiate the road bridge landfall, cement works, oil refineries, petrol storage depots, electricity stations—not to speak of the **Docks**, which require an article to themselves. It has to be admitted that this area of the city is not by any means visitor-friendly: the Dundee Port Authority exhibits stern notices prohibiting admittance except on official business, and dogs are strictly forbidden. This is regrettable, for the dock area was once popular with strollers; indeed there is a route, immediately to the east of the road bridge, which is still shown on the map as 'Marine Parade', but it is barred after a few hundred yards. This was at one time the locus of many joyous crowd scenes including the launch in 1901 of the *Discovery*. Now a pleasant if truncated walkway leads west under the road bridge as far as Discovery Dock. The name 'Marine Parade' sounds rather grandiose (and distinctly un-Dundonian); for that matter so does Riverside Drive: but who nowadays would know the location of the Cowp?

St Mary's Church

When William the Lion, King of Scots, in or around 1190 gave the lordship of Dundee to his brother David (later earl of Huntingdon), there was already a church of 'St Mary's in the Field', adjacent to the nuclear town, but, as the name implies, outwith its boundaries. The legend that Earl David erected a vast church in Dundee as a thank-offering to God on his safe return from the crusades is now largely discredited, but it is still very probable that the establishment of St Mary's was his work. No vestige remains of the original church (reputedly destroyed by Edward I), although the base of the tower is thought to be part of the original structure. The French chronicler Froissart wrote that when Richard II invaded Scotland in 1385 'the English burned Dundee, and spared neither monasteries nor churches, but put all to the flames'.

In the 1440s work was begun on a huge and opulent edifice on the site. The church was rebuilt and extended in cruciform shape; and twenty years later there was added its crowning glory, 'the Old Steeple'; this affectionate name has been current in Dundee for centuries, even though the monument is signposted as 'St Mary's Tower', the name preferred by the purists. 'Old' it certainly is—the most ancient structure surviving in Dundee, and in the words of one scholar 'possibly the highest surviving mediaeval ecclesiastical tower in Scotland'. 'Steeple' is more questionable, although it was not uncommon to use this term (which of course derives from the adjective 'steep') to denote any church tower with or without a spire. Entry to the vast new church was through the great twin doorways at the foot of the Tower, which had been reconstructed in Gothic style on its Norman base. After its completion towards the end of the fifteenth century the whole complex was reckoned to be the largest parish church in Scotland and one of her most magnificent ecclesiastical buildings. But thereafter unfolds a sorry tale of destruction, deterioration, and partial restoration. It began in the mid-sixteenth century with the 'Rough Wooing' by the English, when some of the buildings were badly damaged by fire; and with the coming of the Reformation the church ceased to be collegiate, lost its quasi-cathedral status, and became the parish church of Dundee. Thereafter the building was used by several Protestant congregations; the choir and chancel became variously known as St Mary's, the East Church, and the Old Church; the transept became the Cross Church, and the nave became the Steeple Church. Various alterations to these arrangements took place; one such was in 1588 when 'The bailies and Counsall, finding place of imprisonment devysed for fornicators and adulterers is to be very incommodious, it is concluded that there shall be ane new prison biggit above the volt of St Andro's iyile [aisle], in the eist end of the kirk'.

The Old Steeple miraculously survived the savage attack on the city by Montrose's Royalist army in 1644-5, as it did the 'merciless assault' by Cromwell's General Monck on 1 September 1651. This must have been Dundee's darkest hour. The besiegers are said to have burned wet straw round the base of the Old Steeple with the object of smothering those inside. Governor Lumsden was forced to surrender on terms, despite which he and his defending forces were massacred, along with many of the citizenry who had taken refuge there; his severed head was affixed to a spike on the south west corner of the tower, the remains of it still visible nearly 150 years later during restoration work. Some years later, builders discovered the base of the tower to be thick with human skeletons, confirmation of the circumstances of Monck's bloody victory.

Thereafter the destruction was largely of an accidental nature. In 1789 a new church was built on the site of the former nave and the whole complex was subdivided for use by three congregations (the other two being St Clements and St Mary's). But a spectacular and disastrous fire in 1841 destroyed the former choir and transepts, necessitating a complete reconstruction of all but the Tower. This is how it stands today, apart from a face-lift in the 1960s. A proposed reconstruction of the Tower itself early in the present century involved a restoration of the St Giles-type crown which had supposedly been intended for the Old Steeple but which was never built. The proposal was not approved by the architectural pundits of the day, and so we are left with the modest cape-house which has always graced the top of the Tower.

Most Dundonians of the late twentieth century are quite unaware of the vanished glory and dramatic history of the Old Steeple and the City Churches. The latter are in regular use, and the former is still designated as a museum, but one whose opening times, if any, are a closely-guarded secret. There is scope here for sensitive development: the City of Discovery needs to do a bit of self-rediscovery.

St Roques

Roque (his name is a version of Roche, or rock) was the patron saint of plague victims. It was the practice in Scotland as elsewhere to expel these sufferers from the town and to accommodate them in huts outside the burgh boundary; a chapel would be erected in the vicinity for the benefit of their immortal souls. Such a chapel, accompanied by huts, was to be found at the foot of Blackford Hill in Edinburgh.

This arrangement is exactly paralleled in Dundee, where St Roque had a chapel just outside the East Port (see **Wishart**) on a site known as 'the Sick Mens Yairds'. It is known that there were lodgings for plague victims in the Yards, and the chapel would have been purposely sited nearby. The chapel, known as the Holy Rood, fell into ruin at the time of the Reformation, the last priest having been appointed in 1557. The victims were apparently buried in Roodyards Cemetery, between Ferry Road and Dock Street; 'rood yards' means literally 'enclosure with crosses'.

Curiously, this saint—almost forgotten nowadays—was known in eighteenth century Dundee as 'St Morookie', and a row of houses near the site of the chapel was called 'Semirookie'; this was interpreted by some misguided philologist as 'Summer rookie', but it is undoubtedly an elided version of 'Saint my Roque' (the possessive pronoun being a common interpolation in saints' place-names).

St Roque's chapel stood by the Wallace burn, which ran from the north side of the Law, then veered south-east through the lands of Clepington and, in the words of a nineteenth-century writer, 'entered a deep and narrow den whose grassy banks used to be redolent with wild flowers and shaded by great trees'. He is talking of St Roque's Lane, which would hardly answer to that description nowadays; go and see for yourself if you feel in need of a depressant. The whole area was part of Wallace Craigie, a Scrymgeour domain.

Older Dundonians may remember St Roque's Mill, built by Baxter Brothers in 1889, and others will make an association with St Roque's Garage, a once-thriving concern at the corner of Ward Road and what is now West Marketgait; the reason for commemorating the saint at that particular location is obscure. Most people will however be familiar with the appearance, if not the name, of St Roque's Libary, the only building of any note on the south side of Blackscroft. It was built in 1910 (near the site of the former chapel) as a single-storey French Renaissance pavilion, and the original drawings show it to be set in a formal garden of great elegance. It was funded from part of the Carnegie Library Gift to Dundee, some of the old Blackscroft houses having been cleared when the Town Council acquired the site at the beginning of the century. Recently used as a club but now derelict, this fine building is in a sad state of decrepititude, with crumbling balustrades and blackened stonework. It deserves some human care and attention.

Scourin Burn

You will not find this name on any modern map of Dundee, but it is so central to the city's industrial history that it must be discussed. You may have heard the name from your grandparents, as that of a thoroughfare, before it was replaced by the inappropriate and uninspiring name of Brook Street.

People used sometimes to ask how it came about that the burgh of Dundee developed on its present site and not, for example, on the south side of the river or further down nearer the mouth of the estuary. Surely the answers are obvious—a south-facing slope, a rocky outcrop for a castle, and a Law with a fort for protection. But the early development of manufacturing industry in Dundee is due not to these factors but to the ready supply of water from the streams that drained into the Tay basin in the vicinity of the first settlement.

There is now little evidence of these watercourses, which have long since been culverted; but they included the Tod's burn ('tod' being Scots for fox) and the more sizeable Dens burn and its tributary the Wallace burn (see separately under **Dens** and **Wallace**). The old name Scourin Burn, or 'cleansing burn', probably referred to the process of waulking and scouring yarn; the burn apparently had in pre-industrial days the alternative names of the Friars burn and the Mausie burn. It rose somewhere to the west of the Law, flowed down the line of Brook Street and Guthrie Street and along Ward Road to Meadowside where it was apparently dammed so as to increase its head of water.

The Burnhead, at the top of what is now Commercial Street, was the point where the Dens Burn and the Scourin Burn met, both having taken a wide sweep from different sides of the Law; and the combined stream flowed to the river on a line parallel to Commercial Street '...down the slopes of the Castle Rock, driving the Malt Mills, which were common property'; the stream also powered a thread mill until around 1790. A contemporary writer considered these streams to be possibly 'the most valuable in Scotland in proportion to their volume of water...they supply the greater part of the steam-engines in the town; and from their upper sources water is carted to town, and sold at the rate of 6 gallons a penny'. The overworked little stream joined the estuary at a creek situated at the intersection of Gellatly Street and the Seagate.

Maps of nineteenth-century Dundee show concentrations of manufacturing industry along the courses of the Scourin Burn and its companion streams. Housing was run up nearby to accommodate the workers; and it could be said that Dundee's early urban development was dictated by the presence of these little watercourses. Most of the factories have now gone, or have been adapted for non-industrial use, and the substandard housing has been cleared. A small section of the culverted Scourin burn can still be seen running under the floorboards of Verdant Works, built in 1833 and situated between Milne Street and Guthrie Street; but it is many a long year since the burn did any serious scouring.

Scrymgeour

This surname, although not commemorated in any street or building, must be among the most important in Dundee's history. The founder of the family, Alexander Scrymgeour, had compelled the English to surrender the castle of Dundee, and for his signal efforts in the cause of national independence received from William Wallace in 1298 'a grant of the hereditary office of Constable of the castle and of the town of Dundee' together with a gift of some adjoining lands. At the same time he was confirmed in his family's hereditary appointment as standard-bearer of Scotland, and this honour continued in the Scrymgeour line long after the office of Constable had ceased to exist at the end of the seventeenth century. Henry Scrymger, of a cadet branch of the family, was one of the greatest Greek scholars of the sixteenth century.

Scrimgeour was pronounced 'scrimmager' and means what it says—a skirmisher, or in the words of the sixteenth-century Dundee-born historian Hector Boece, 'ane scharp fechter', and the family sustained this reputation. Alexander Scrymgeour appears to have owned the lands of Balbeuchlie ('crozier place', near Auchterhouse) and Templeton ('templar land') near Birkhill, and his descendants acquired the lands of **Dudhope** where they built a fortalice to replace the ancient castle of Dundee (see under **Castle**). The family figured prominently in Scotland's roll of honour: one of them fell at the battle of Halidon Hill in 1333 and another at Harlaw in 1411. They became viscounts of Dudhope in 1641; the second viscount was mortally wounded at Marston Moor in 1643 fighting in the parliamentary army for 'Christ's Crown and Covenant'; a generation later his son, having reverted to the the traditional royalist beliefs of the Scrymgeours, took up arms on behalf of Charles II at the battle of Worcester and after the Restoration was elevated to the earldom of Dundee. The title did not however remain long in the family, for the last of them died without issue in the direct line in 1688 and the Scrymgeours were 'unjustly spoiled of their honours and inheritance'. It was not until the 1950s that Scrimgeour-Wedderburn of Birkhill in Fife was restored to the earldom (see also **Wedderburn**).

At the time of the second viscount's death the Scrymgeour family held extensive properties in and around Dundee including (apart from Dudhope) Balunie, East Ferry, Duntrune, Baldovie, Linlathen, Craigie, Baldovan, part of Strathmartine, Balruddery and Benvie—most of Dundee's hinterland, in fact, as a glance at the map will confirm. The family also had strong aristocratic connections by marriage, and their influence in the politics of the city and country was correspondingly great.

But Scrymgeour had long been a common surname in Dundee, and one of its bearers, of non-aristocratic origin, came to play an important part in the city's political history in the twentieth century. Edwin ('Neddy') Scrymgeour had been a pacifist during the Kaiser's war and a member of the Independent Labour Party, but his political beliefs were strongly guided by his Christian faith and his antipathy towards the evil and corruption of his time. Of these evils, alcohol appeared to him to be among the worst, and he stood for parliament as a member of a home-made Prohibitionist Party. Dundee in Victorian times had been a stronghold of radical Liberalism, a fact which caused Winston Churchill to view it as a safe seat for life. He realised his mistake in 1922, when Scrymgeour defeated him at the polls by a comfortable margin. Scrymgeour was an immensely popular figure in Dundee, and went on to a further election victory in 1924, although by this time he was helped by tactical voting on the part of Liberals and Conservatives who considered him preferable to a Labour member. Scrymgeour's career came to an end with the formation of a National Government in 1931; a sardonic letter to the *Courier* ran—'Let it be known through the land that we in Dundee, one of the hardest boozing cities…have turned a Prohibitionist out of Parliament'. Scrymgeour lived on for many years, dying in obscurity in 1947.

There are no Scrymgeour street-names in Dundee, but the University when expanding its Law Faculty had the sensitivity to rename the old Training College 'The Scrymgeour Building'—with of course no reference to Prohibition.

Seagate

The Seagate was at the heart of the mediaeval burgh, with the Castle at its west end and the Seagate Port at the east. In addition to town houses for the nobility it contained the following, established in the time of Robert the

Bruce: the ancient tolbooth, where the courts and councils met, where tolls and customs were collected, burghal justice administered and offenders imprisoned; the tron or public weigh-bridge (but it was a beam and not a platform); and the market cross, where deals were done and proclamations made. The author of the *First Statistical Account of Dundee* (1793) tells us that 'in the broadest part of the Seagate remains of the ancient cross were still to be seen; and by marks in the present causeway its situation is still distinguished'—but no longer so. Near the site of the tolbooth there used to be pointed out the spot where 'in times of ignorance and bigotry Grizzel Jaffray was burnt for witchcraft'.

The Seagate never lost its importance as a strategic thoroughfare (which it still retains) but there are no mediaeval relics to be seen, and even the site of the Port is a matter for conjecture; also, after the reclamation of land for the docks, it became remote from the sea, thus to some extent losing its *raison d'être*. The administrative centre had started moving westwards in the fourteenth century; the market cross, the tolbooth and the tron were all transferred to the Marketgate (the old name for the High Street); the East Port and its environs never fully recovered from the poundings received from Montrose's army in 1644 and the even more severe depredations six years later of General Monck, during the disastrous siege and sacking of the city; and although the eighteenth century Seagate still had one or two fine town houses, with long rigs on the site of Trades Lane and the bus station, these were soon swallowed up by the whaling warehouses and factories of the coming industrial era. In the later Victorian period, the Seagate was graced by several substantial bonded warehouses, which have now been sensibly adapted for other purposes including private housing and a printmaker's workshop; but the present Seagate, while it has improved since the days when it was a slowly-moving car park, still presents a somewhat austere face to the world.

Near the corner of Seagate and Commercial Street is one of Dundee's few remaining cinemas—from the outside, somewhat anonymous but in fact part of the Cannon chain. It is hard to believe now that in the heyday of the silver screen there were at least 37 cinemas in the city, most of them with twice-weekly changes of programme; it was possible even for the very choosy to have a week of excellent evening entertainment for the cost of one road-bridge toll. Of course one realises that picture-houses (to use the old Dundee term) are no longer dream palaces, and that to enter any cinema nowadays is to risk encountering a grim reality that is far from entertaining. Nevertheless there is no harm in recalling that on the site of this particular cinema stood 'Her Majesty's Theatre and Opera House', a bijou Victorian building which opened in 1885, once the home of visiting companies such as D'Oyly Carte and Carl Rosa Opera, Wilson Barrett Repertory and glamorous music-hall and variety shows. One recalls elderly relatives enthusing over Henry Irving's performance in *The Bells* in this very theatre. But the Dundee theatre-going public has always been a fickle one, and in the '30s the house was given over to movies and, with a return to a male monarchy, renamed The Majestic. A disastrous fire in 1941 was followed five or six years later by a complete rebuild; and however functional may be the auditorium which replaced it there is little that is majestic about its external appearance.

Leading from the Seagate to the Murraygate is an alley, until quite recently graced with old-fashioned 'shoppies', and earlier (hard to believe) with stately mansions, but now just a canyon between huge buildings. It is called Horse Wynd—why, one wonders, because horses at one time used every Dundee street with the possible exception of the Hilltown. There is a story of a Dundee street-sweeper of bygone days who overheard an American visitor remarking, 'Say, this is a one-horse town'. To which the scaffie dolefully added, 'Ye widnae say that if ye'd meh joab'.

Sinderins

To 'sinder' in Scots is to part. The ideal number of children in a family was four—'twa tae fecht, ane tae sinder and ane tae rin and tell'. The Sinderins in Dundee refers to a parting of the ways or sundering of the roads, one going east along the present Perth Road and the other up the Hawkhill; the name, although not of any great antiquity, presents a good opportunity for discussing the original street system in the town centre, now obliterated by the ring road and one-way traffic arrangements.

There were basically two means of access to the city on its western side, one on the south and one on the north. The southern was the Nethergait (the 'lower street') and the northern was the **Overgait** ('upper street'). These two routes were at one time of equal importance, but with the development of turnpikes in the nineteenth century the less narrow route along Perth Road acquired a monopoly of the traffic. A Victorian gazetteer describes it nicely: '…one great line of street—somewhat sinuous, but over most of the distance not much off the straight line—it stretches from west to east, near and along the shore, under the names of Perth-road, Nethergate, High street, Seagate, and the Crofts, nearly 1¾ mile'.

An earlier name for the Nethergait was the Fluckergate: current from the twelfth century, it recalls the route of the fishermen who made a living from the catching of flukes, a species of flatfish related to the turbot and of some commercial importance. Flucker was a familiar surname in Dundee in the late mediaeval period; and anglers still fish for flukes in the Tay. As the town spread westwards the more euphonious name of Nethergate came into use, complete with its misleading spelling, for 'gate' in this context of course means 'way', and not a portal. The Nethergate at that time did not stretch beyond the gateway known as the Barras ('barrier') Port, near the end of the present Long Wynd; Springfield and Westfield were rural villages until the beginning of the nineteenth century. Before the reclamation of the estuarine shore the houses on the southern side of the Nethergate had a river frontage with attractive views. The coming of the railways and the development of the marshalling yards ruined the landscape.

The continuation of the Nethergate to the east, as far as the junction of **Murraygate** and **Seagate**, was the Mercatgait; the name was revived in the form 'Marketgait' to designate the inner ring road, a somewhat misleading nomenclature since it scarcely impinges at any point on the line of the original Mercatgait. In the eighteenth century the Mercatgait became dignified with the name High Street; this is where the action was, and a contemporary writer commented on the fine new market place for butchery meat, a shambles or slaughter place, and 'an elegant hall for the Nine Incorporated Trades'. These developments were praised as giving 'real ornament to all around'; and the prize went to the Town House, designed by William Adam and finished in 1732. This fine building included the town gaol, but its chief merit apart from its classical exterior lay in the splendid suite of rooms at first-floor level, reached by a fine oval staircase. As often the case in Dundee, however, the building was of inferior stone and soon acquired a somewhat dingy appearance. Even more unfortunate was its situation: surrounded by a clutter of of buildings not cleared away until the Victorian era, it was described in 1799 as having been 'set down in a hole fitted only for a hog's stye, and what is to be much lamented, it is one of those capital blunders which cannot, without immense expense, be now remedied'. Had this percipient writer lived for another century or so he would have had the melancholy satisfaction of seeing the destruction of what had been potentially one of the finest buildings in Scotland of its time: it was demolished in the early 1930s to make way for the City Square. And he was right also about the immense expense (see **Caird**).

Stannergate

Stannergate Road is the modern name of an old highway which runs parallel to the Ferry Road, but at a lower level; starting from West Ferry it leads towards the docks where at some indeterminate point it merges with

Camperdown Street. Such words of explanation would not have been necessary a century ago, when Dundonians would have been familiar with 'the Stannergait' as being part of the coastal route to Arbroath; and the preferred spelling 'gait' would indicate that the reference was to a way and not a gate or district. The prefix incorporates the old Scots word stanners, meaning 'shingle', and it may be that the Stannergate was the track used by citizens requiring river gravel for building or other purposes. So the name, although recorded in charters of the sixteenth century, is of no great antiquity compared with some others in and around Dundee.

In the nineteenth century the name Stannergate acquired some fame in scholarly circles as being the place where a number of archaeological finds were made; these included some coffins with human remains, urns of unburnt clay and other evidences of human occupation, thought to be round about the period of the Roman occupation. Even more interesting however was the exposing in 1878 of a huge shell-bed or 'kitchen midden' which contained a large number of shells of edible molluscs, porpoise bones, antlers, stone implements and other evidences of an early colony of fishermen. These finds were made during excavations which took place between the railway and the shore in connection with the construction of a new dock; and the fact that the shell-bed was discovered beneath twelve feet of topsoil (deposited probably as the result of a landslide) indicates that it belonged to a much earlier period than that of the Romans.

The shell-midden lay on a rocky gravel bed some thirty feet above the present sea-level; this is taken as evidence that it belongs to the Mesolithic period, when it is known that the Tay estuary was subject to considerable and prolonged flooding. A few years later a second shell midden was discovered on the eastern slope of Forthill in Broughty Ferry, half a mile from the present shoreline. The extent and depth of the middens indicated occupation over a long period of years, possibly into the Neolithic period and the Bronze age. These discoveries put the Stannergate on a par with Tentsmuir (three miles away on the Fife coast) as one of the first sites in northern Britain known to have been settled by humans. Nothing of course remains to be seen above ground; and motorists negotiating the busy traffic of East Dock Street are unlikely to be aware that they are traversing what may be the landfall of some of the earliest immigrants from contintental Europe, more than six thousand years before the birth of Christ.

Stobsmuir and Stobswell

A stob is a wooden stake or post, a familiar sight in the rural landscape; the word features in many Scottish place-names. Stobs in Roxburgh means exactly what it says, and Stobo is a contraction of 'stob-hole'; Stobcross and Stobhill in Glasgow, and Stobhall on the Tay all have fairly obvious meanings. The word stob was borrowed into Gaelic, giving such mountain names as Stobinian ('stob peaks') and Stob Coire an Lochain ('stob of the corrie of the little loch'). Nearer home we find Stobsmuir and Stobswell, both in the Pitkerro Road area and clearly referring to some posts or other whose existence and significance are now forgotten.

The suffix of Stobsmuir recalls the fact that this place was outside the old town boundary, and was indeed open moorland. Such places were frequently used for holding fairs, and there is evidence that fairs took place in Dundee as early as the thirteenth century. They were intended mainly for the selling of cattle and horses and other more exotic wares, and were free from the restrictions commonly enforced in respect of the official marketplace. Some of them were hiring fairs for agricultural labourers and domestic servants who were seeking a job-change, and the Stobs fair, which dates from the eighteenth century, was of this latter kind. Unruly conduct was often to be found, and the city officers had to be called in to supervise the 'fechtin fairs' of which Stobsmuir was one of the more notorious.

The 'fechtin' at Stobs fair was, to begin with, of a harmless nature, the result of high spirits and doubtless of an excess of alcohol (the adjacent Stobs Toll-house was 'licensed to retail beer, spirits and ale'); but in July 1809 the *Dundee Advertiser* had to report an outbreak of mayhem. This was the period of the Napoleonic wars, and it appears that a press-gang party from the 25th Regiment stationed at Dudhope Castle met with some resistance from a band of young men attending the fair who were reluctant to be pressed into His Majesty's service. A pitched battle followed, resulting in two deaths and two cases of severe wounding. The civic authorities however seem to have regarded this as no more than par for the course, and took no action; the fair subsequently degenerated into an annual affray, and in 1814 the *Advertiser* noted that 'This Fair has always concluded with a list of broken heads, and too frequently with a list of killed and wounded'. But eventually things got so bad that in 1824, after a gang fight in which a totally innocent man was murdered and his brother grievously wounded, the authorities at last took action to clean up the fair at Stobsmuir. Our own century has no monopoly of violence.

The traditional fairs were replaced later in the nineteenth century by travelling fairs and circuses, designed purely for entertainment, and taking place on different sites such as Gussie Park and Riverside Park. Judging by its name, Fairmuir was probably the site of one of the early fairs, but it continued its function into the era of fun-fairs.

Stobsmuir's other claim to fame was that its ponds for a time during the nineteenth century acted as a trunk mains for the city's water supply; the name Stobswell probably reflects an earlier hydraulic function (see **Wellgate**). Not unsurprisingly the Stobsmuir water was highly unsatisfactory; it was only with the appointment in the1870s of a qualified water engineer, and the construction of proper reservoirs at Clatto and Lintrathen, that Dundonians had a decent water-supply. The 'swannie ponds' as they were known to the children of the locality are still used by them for 'messing about in boats'; but open-air ice-skating belongs to those far-off days when we had regular seasons and not just a series of arbitrary weather-fronts.

Stobswell appears in the directories only under Stobswell Road, an insignificant continuation of Dundonald Street; but, as every Dundee person knows, it is also the name given to the area at the intersection of Albert Street, Forfar Road, Dura Street and Pitkerro Road. Stobswell bakery is the HQ of Wallace (Land o' Cakes) Ltd., which once employed more than a hundred pairs of hands and fed countless more mouths (see **Wallace**). This multicultural district was also the home of Dundee's first cinema, the 'Stobswell Cinema and Theatre', built in 1910 and later renamed the Ritz, a name whose appropriateness was not immediately obvious; but along with most of the city's cinematic and other glories, it vanished in the 1960s.

Strathmartine

There is something of a mystery about this name. The *strath* bit is all right, being the common Gaelic term for a broad valley (which exactly describes the terrain through which the Dighty Water flows). But in place-nomenclature the term *strath* is invariably followed by the name of the stream which drains it (like Strathtay or Strathardle) or by an adjective describing the valley itself (like Strathmore—'the great valley'). Why should the name Strathmartine be an apparently unique formation?

Martin is clearly a personal name, and there is a well-known local legend of someone called Martin slaying a dragon which was molesting the females of the neighbourhood. Whatever the truth of the legend, its antiquity is corroborated by the neighbouring place-name of Baldragon, which means in Gaelic 'dragon stead', and by the presence of a standing stone near Balkello farm (shown on the Ordnance Survey maps as Martin's Stone) depicting a horseman and a serpent. This is still pointed out as the place where Martin traditionally carried out his deed of valour. He has in recent times been referred to as 'St Martin', but there seems to be no foundation for his saintly status: he was more likely to have been a Pictish warrior.

The name Strathmartine probably came about in this way. The valley was earlier known as 'Strathdichty', which is quite unexceptionable (see under **Dighty**); but the name and fame of Martin (or Martine) must have led to its adoption as a suffix in place of Dighty. It may be noted that the village of Strathmartine (which came into being in 1791) used to be referred to as 'Kirkton of Strathmartine' and now appears on the map as Bridgefoot (after the bridge which was built in 1795); Strathmartine Castle was somewhat earlier, and Martin's Stone is much nearer to the castle than to the village. This seems to confirm that Strathmartine was not originally a settlement-name but was descriptive of the whole of that part of what we might call 'the strath of the Dighty'.

The earls of Strathmartine were a powerful local family, with an imposing town-house on the site of the present City Chambers (demolished along with the Town House in the 1930s), and this is possibly why the main thoroughfare leading from the Hilltown to the Sidlaws was called Strathmartine Road. Older citizens will remember this road as the route of the Downfield tram, with its terminus at Baldovan Road. You would have to be very old, however, to remember that Downfield was once a country hamlet, on land belonging to the Ogilvy lairds of Baldovan; it was developed for housing in the early nineteenth century, being conveniently situated on the old Caledonian railway line to Newtyle. A nineteenth-century guidebook describes Downfield as 'a village that has sprung into importance within recent years, and is fast becoming a favourite residence of the middle class merchants and business men, who here find a healthy rural retreat for their families away from the smoke and bustle of the reeking town'. Downfield maintained its rustic atmosphere until the end of the Second World War, but is now in the centre of a large conurbation marking Dundee's principal expansion to the north. The old Kirkton of Strathmartine remains a country village, but Strathmartine Road now extends far beyond the former City Boundary and it would be an optimist who would believe that urban development will not follow.

Tay

There is no river in Europe—possibly in the world—which is so beautiful for its entire length as the Tay. Rising on the slopes of Ben Lui in Perthshire and joining the North Sea at the bar between Carnoustie and Tentsmuir, it flows through some of the loveliest scenery in Scotland; and if you insist that its waters are somewhat muddy as it passes the Stannergate you have only to look up the estuary to see a view that has brought a lump to the throat of many a returning exile.

The name of this noble river is among the oldest in Scotland—older than English or Gaelic or Pictish. Older indeed than, and unconnected with, the name Dundee. The experts (for the time being at least) seem to agree that Tay comes from a hypothetical Indo-European root *ta*, meaning 'to melt, dissolve or flow', and point to other British water-names such as Thames, Tamar and several others; there are also continental river-names such as Taggia and Taverone in Italy which confirm the theory that Tay is probably a pre-Celtic element.

Dundee owes everything to the Tay—for good or ill, because as well as being a waterway giving easy access to the heart of Scotland for peaceful commercial purposes it has been a gateway for invading forces, mainly from England. It would be pleasant but not quite accurate to say that the city has discharged its debt to the river; the shoreline is disfigured by ignoble buildings, and time after time the opportunity has been lost to create a riverside environment that is worthy of Dundee's noble setting. The industrial developments around the docks are of long-standing, and unavoidable for a town that has always been a thriving seaport; but the area between the old Craig Pier and the railway bridge has been subjected to insensitive treatment over the decades, first with the railway marshalling yards and later with not very sightly mega-stores. Even the Esplanade, once a pleasant promenade, has become an untidy mess (which one hopes is only temporary). It is just as well that the river itself is apparently indestructible, and indeed for all its ill-treatment remains the cleanest major estuary in Europe.

It is natural that the name Tay should have generated many other Dundee names. Let us pass over the fatuous board-room name of 'Tayside' Region, which is discussed under **Angus** and is now obsolete, and turn to names such as Tay Street and Tay Square, among the bonniest parts of Georgian and Early Victorian Dundee. South Tay Street was begun in 1792, the purpose being to link Hawkhill with the Nethergate; the later addition of North Tay Street carried travellers to the developing industrial suburb of Lochee. But North Tay Street has been gobbled up by the ring road, which does not anyway connect with South Tay Street. Roads that lead nowhere tend to become forgotten, like jokes which lack a punchline, and the remaining Tay Street is not what it was. The pleasant Regency frontage of the eastern side is still to be admired, but the poor-quality Dundee stone resists any smartening up process, and the present rash of 'To Let' signs is a reminder that the recession may not yet be over. Tay Square has lost some of its old world charm, but is compensated by the exciting Repertory Theatre. Now that the derelict garage at the foot of the street has been removed there may be scope for upgrading the whole of this once fashionable area.

Other 'Tay' names abound. This is not the place to discuss the Tay

Bridges, nor the various Tay Terraces, Parks, Views and Courts which line the river front from Invergowrie to Monifieth. **Tayport** has an entry to itself. The Tay Hotel deserves a mention however; known to generations as Mathers Hotel, it occupies a commanding site at the foot of Union Street which was convenient for all three adjacent railway stations (Dundee East, Dundee West and Taybridge, of which only the last-named remains). It has recently been restored to its former appearance of Victorian grandeur and prosperity, but can hardly derive much satisfaction from the presence of its oversized and ill-sited neighbour Tayside House, which must be due for re-naming at the very least.

Tayport

The name of Tayport is quite modern. In mediaeval times it was known as Portincraig, which is in fact an approximate rendering into Scots of the Gaelic *port-na-creige* ('port of the crag'—probably a reference to Scotscraig, which is known to have been a beacon hill). For good measure the prefix 'ferry' was added in modern times, and the place was for long known as Ferry-Port-on-Craig. The name was contracted (so the story goes) because it was too long to print on train tickets; these were being issued by the railway company when the village became a railhead on the Fife side for travellers between Dundee and Fife (linking with Edinburgh and the south). We never think about it nowadays, but if any place deserved the name of 'Tay Port', it is surely Dundee itself. As it is, we have our revenge by refer-ring to Tayport (with Newport and Wormit) as 'Dundee across the Water'.

An account of the ferry services across the Tay is given under **New-port**; but from an early time boats also ran between Port-on-Craig and Broughty, the narrowest part of the estuary. So closely were the two vil-lages linked that for a time the Angus terminal was known as North Ferry and the Fife terminal as South Ferry. Indeed the two terminals sometimes shared the same name, as did those at Queensferry: Broughty was occa-sionally styled Port-on-Craig, and this is probably the correct rendering of *Partan Craig* ('crab rock') sometimes said to have been an old name for the original fishing hamlet (see **Broughty**).

During the railway expansion in the 1840s, the Dundee-Newport and the Broughty-Tayport ferries were acquired and run by two different rail-way companies. In 1846 the Edinburgh and Northern Railway bought the latter crossing to enable them to expand the railway to the north; a rail ferry, like the one between Granton and Burntisland, started in 1851. It was an elaborate and ingenious arrangement: flying bridges allowed wagons to run from rail lines on the dock onto those on the boats—an early form of

RORO rail ferry, in effect. In these pre-Tay Bridge days there were no passenger services on this particular crossing; but when these were introduced a few years later the rail journey from Edinburgh to Dundee involved de-training at Tayport and entraining at Broughty Ferry. When Charles Kingsley had to travel from St Andrews to the British Association meetings in Dundee in 1867 it took him several hours to accomplish what is now a twenty-minute journey.

In 1801 the population of the entire parish of Ferryport-on-Craig was less than a thousand; it had trebled by the end of the century. There was apparently a castle on the shore, corresponding to the similar one at Broughty, but the site was built over when the burgh extended to the west in the 1850s. Tayport is essentially a nineteenth-century creation, and its independent existence might well have ceased with the coming of the first rail bridge; to some extent this did happen, when Wormit and Newport became dormitories for Dundee's rail-commuters. But Tayport always differed from its neighbour Newport in having its basis in industry: at one time there were in Tayport a jute mill, two linen factories, saw mills, a timber yard and a foundry. In the years following 1918, Dundee Corporation acquired the Scotscraig estate with the intention of developing its river frontage for shipbuilding and other major industrial development. This never materialised, and Tayport remains a very attractive place to live; except possibly for **Monifieth** it is now Dundee's biggest dormitory suburb. Further small-scale development continues, not all of it based on commuterdom.

The Tayport ferry-crossing was superseded by the first Tay rail bridge, but was revived for eight years after the collapse of the bridge in 1879. The passenger service from Tayport to Broughty Ferry ran until 1939, and a favourite jaunt in our grandparents' day used to involve crossing to Newport, walking east along the braes to Tayport and taking the ferry crossing to Broughty. Although pleasure steamers continued to operate for some time afterwards, coach tours eventually supplanted steamers in the public's affections.

When you survey Tayport from Broughty Ferry, particularly in certain lights, the crossing seems quite narrow. Indeed, the Amphibians used to swim it regularly from Broughty Harbour (nowadays, one imagines, a stomach pump would be a necessary adjunct). It may seem paradoxical that, in the way the river crossings have developed, Tayport is nowadays more isolated from Broughty than at any time since the later Middle Ages.

Thomson

D.C. Thomson & Co Ltd is one of the last of the great Dundee dynasties and probably the longest-surviving large family firm in the city. The story begins at Pittenweem in 1817 with the birth of William Thomson, son of a seafaring man. The young William was apprenticed to a draper in Anstruther, whence he moved to Dundee to start a clothier's business in Union Street. He began to make his name in the wholesale side of the business and then diversified into other commercial ventures, one of which was shipping. The formation in the 1850s of a large trading fleet called the Thomson Line made his name, and its success made his fortune.

One of William Thomson's many other business interests was journalism, and there was no shortage in Dundee of ailing newspapers ready to be taken over. The Dundee press in the early nineteenth century was of the radical persuasion; and the *Courier* had been founded in 1816 in opposition to the left-wing *Advertiser* (see under **Leng**). When Thomson took over the *Courier* in 1884 he became proprietor of a paper with a seventy-year-long tradition of conservatism in politics; and this doubtless suited his own views. William Thomson and his sons Frederick and David, along with their respective wives, formed the family firm; it was David's middle name of Couper which produced the initials in D.C. Thomson Ltd; since then all the directors have carried the Thomson surname.

The erection of the Courier Building in Meadowside in 1902 was a public demonstration of the firm's strength, and the Thomson merger with the Leng press in 1906 was more in the nature of a takeover by the former. Another merger occurred after the General Strike in 1926, when the *Courier* and the *Advertiser* became one, giving Thomsons a monopoly of Dundee newspapers. Not only newspapers but periodicals also: some of the old Leng titles such as *My Weekly* and *The People's Friend*, with their politically radical outlook, were gradually transformed into couthy or genteel women's magazines of a totally non-political nature but with a built-in conservative stance.

It was in 1920 that D.C. Thomson entered the world of children's journalism with the launch of the *Adventure* comic, the first of a string of papers for older children; (it was said that publication was partly intended to provide work for ex-employees returning from the war). In 1937 the *Dandy* appeared, followed a year later by the *Beano*. The Dundee intelligentsia at first disapproved of these apparently rather mindless comics as reading matter for their offspring, but eventually came to recognize their concealed artistry and their essential wholesomeness. Later still, academic theses have been written on Dudley D. Watkins, the inspired artist who first drew Oor Wullie and other characters of world-wide fame. It is ironic that the Thomson comics, having attained respectability in the minds of adults, are likely to be supplanted in youthful affections by American-style strip cartoons, not to speak of videos. The days of Desperate Dan may after all be numbered.

The Thomson press has of course had its critics, although the extent of its commitment to right-wing causes has probably been exaggerated. The story of David Thomson's feud with Churchill is well-known, but it should be remembered that in 1922 the latter was a Liberal with a strong radical streak. It is probably true that Thomson was the cause of Churchill's vow never more to set foot in Dundee, and certainly during David Thomson's lifetime Churchill's name did not again appear in the columns of the *Courier*; but the belief that it was Churchill's personal animosity that was behind Dundee's lack of barrage-balloon protection in 1939 is mere legend. (Churchill as a war-leader was of course a different matter, and he had no stronger supporter than the Dundee press). Thomson's anti-union stance was part of the bitter legacy of the General Strike of 1926; it has been resented more by politicans than by the Thomson employees, for whom job-security and good working conditions have, it would seem, provided some compensation for lack of unionised protection and for non-union wage rates.

Dundee has always held the firm of D.C. Thomson in respect and sometimes in affection. It is odd that a Labour-voting populace should cheerfully buy the right-wing *Courier* day after day, year after year, and that its Conservative views should have apparently had little or no effect on the voting patterns of its readership. But papers such as *The Sunday Post* have probably had considerable social impact, and despite recent changes in editorial policy continue to uphold the so-called family values. Some Dundonians may gripe about the Thomsons and their monopoly of the local press, but most would go to great lengths to secure the continuation of their beloved home-grown *Courier* and its companion papers.

Union

Few political debates have gone on for quite as long as that which still rages over the merits or otherwise of the union of the Scottish and English parliaments which took place in 1707. The possible benefits of union were apparent to most Scots even before 1707, and, despite the allegations at the time of English bribery and Scottish self-interest, there was a certain inevitability about the whole process. Yet the immediate effects were not encouraging: Scotland's trading activities became open to English competition, and increased taxation was more in evidence than were the promised concessions. As early as 1713 there was a motion before the Lords (narrowly defeated) to dissolve the union, and the rising of 1715 derived much of its support from dissatisfaction with the deal that had taken place eight years previously. For well over a century the Union remained a constant political issue with its strong defenders as well as its detractors.

But this does not quite account for the rash of Union-names that were given to streets, buildings, bridges and canals in the nineteenth century, when, it might have been thought, the Union was well-established and too fundamental a feature of the Scottish polity to generate much topical fervour, far less to require to be defended. Part of the answer must be that the Union, initially speculative, remained to some extent precarious (perhaps it has never been more uncertain than it is today). Civic and municipal authorities were enjoined by Government to emphasise the one-ness of the United Kingdom, and every possible occasion was to be taken to celebrate its perceived benefits in a public manner (much in the same way as the army holds Queen's Birthday parades). At a more mundane level, it may be added that practically every Scottish city acquired its Union Street (starting with Aberdeen, the most famous, in 1801), and the term 'Union' became part of the stock-in-trade of those responsible for municipal nomenclature.

Dundee is quite remarkable in this respect. As well as Union Street, there were two Union Places, a Union Hall in the market place (originally known as the Trades Hall, demolished in the street-widening undertakings of 1871) and Union Mount, a villa on Perth Road which formed the nucleus of University College Dundee and now houses the Economics Department. Lochee for a time enjoyed an independence in street-names, and some of them were forcibly changed in 1907 to avoid duplication with Dundee: casualties included Union Place (which became Cobden Street, after the free-trader politician) and Union Street (which became Bright Street after his friend John Bright). Union Street in Maxwelltown became Carnegie Street (after the steel magnate turned philanthropist) and yet another Union Street became (less interestingly) Charles Lane. The name *Union* was even given to the first ferry steamer between Dundee and Newport in 1821.

Union Street in the centre of Dundee was designed in the 1820s as part of the plans to improve and open up the mediaeval heart of the city; of these plans **Reform** Street is the most notable result, but poor old Union Street never quite made the grade. It was intended to have a uniform row of ground-floor shops with quality flats above; and although this was achieved to some degree, the stonework in course of time took on a shabby appearance. The southern half (South Union Street) vanished with the coming of the road bridge, taking with it the pleasing vista down to the river. The once-stylish Royal Hotel has been reconstructed, but not as a hotel, and although there are still a few old-established shops, the sense of being a stone's throw from the water's edge is no longer present. Union Street used to be thronged with pedestrians, for it had to cope twice daily with the Fife commuters: not only the train travellers from Tayport and points west, but also the foot passengers disembarking at Craig Pier from the ferry (universally known as 'the Fifie'). It also afforded a pleasurable stroll to the esplanade in an atmosphere relatively free of traffic noise and fumes.

Valentine

In the Westfield area of the Perth Road there is an unpretentious eighteenth-century building known as Valentine House. The once shiny brass plate has now gone, and one would not give the place a second glance: but it was formerly the home of one of Dundee's most famous and flourishing concerns, namely 'Messrs Valentine, Art Publishers of Dundee'.

In 1825 John Valentine set up a small business making engraved wooden blocks for the printing of linen. His son James joined him in the business in 1832, after apparently having trained as a portrait painter; James not only brought artistic qualities to the enterprise but also a great amount of flair and initiative, and from being a self-styled lithographer and printer he set up his stall as a photographer and 'fancy stationer'. A studio was opened in the Murraygate, at first for portraiture but later also for the landscape views for which the firm became, in the words of its familiar logo, 'Famous Throughout the World'. Queen Victoria, sharing the general enthusiasm for this new art form, commissioned James to produce a series of views of Highland scenery and granted him a warrant as 'Photographer to the Queen'.

William Valentine, grandson of the founder and son of James, continued his father's pioneering work in photography and also expanded the firm's business interests into England. The era of the picture postcard was at hand, and it was to be Valentines who led the field. With the ending of the government monopoly of postcards in 1894 the days of mass-production had arrived, and the Dundee firm's photographic repertoire extended to 20,000 views not only of Bonnie Scotland but also of England, Wales, Ireland and Norway. The firm also bought and distributed photographs from other agencies including Hollywood film stars. Valentines' pay-roll of about a hundred (which numbered among its outworkers such celebrities as Mabel Lucie Atwell) increased tenfold in the same number of years, and the firm's activities spread over half the world with branches in North America, Australia and South Africa. After the turn of the century Valentines of Dundee became one of the largest publishers of postcards in the world.

The postcard boom began to wane at the time of the Great War, although it revived sufficiently in the thirties to justify the firm opening another factory on the Kingsway. Meanwhile Valentines in Perth Road and under the management of a new generation, began to diversify into greeting cards and calendars; these were not photographically produced but were hand-coloured by an army of deft-fingered Dundee lassies. Theirs was a highly skilled occupation, and the employees were of white-collar status (or whatever is the female equivalent); conspicuously well dressed, when seen leaving their work in residential Perth Road to proceed homewards up Millar's Wynd, they were nicknamed 'Valies dallies'.

But the days of family firms are usually numbered, and so it was with Valentines. The photographic studio closed in 1928, and there was a marked decline in the artistic quality of the firm's output. Early deaths of members of the family deprived the firm of some of its enterprising zest; colour photography was an innovation that passed Valentines by. Postcard publishing stopped for ever in 1970, the stocks were sold and the company was taken over a decade later and the Dundee manufactory withdrawn.

The good news is that the entire Valentine archive, comprising some 50,000 topographical views, was presented to the University of St Andrews where it has been carefully curated and has been the subject of several attractive exhibitions. What is more, Andrew Valentine, the last member of the family to have worked in the business, is now chairman of his own company, Valentine Marketing Limited; he is to work with the University in opening the archive for commercial use, and will sell selected prints, postcards and greetings cards on a world-wide basis. So those of us who remember dispatching Valentines' scenic views of Scotland to selected friends during holiday seasons of long ago may be able in some measure to relive those happy days.

Victoria

Queen Victoria's visit to Dundee in 1844 was the first such by a reigning monarch for almost two centuries, and the occasion was marked by the erection of a massive gateway at the dock where she disembarked; a wooden arch was later replaced by an elaborate erection in stone. Considering that the monarch's visit lasted less than one hour—she was on her way to Blair Atholl, this being during her pre-Balmoral phase—perhaps the tribute was slightly on the generous side. The Royal Arch and the docks were notable features of bygone Dundee, when the seafaring nature of the city was much more in evidence than it is now: craft were anchored within a stone's throw of the Caird Hall, maritime clobber lay about the quaysides, and the shoreside pubs were frequented by exotic-looking seamen from the Indian sub-continent. Although Victoria Dock is still in existence, most of the physical evidence of Dundee *qua* seaport was cleared to make way for the landfall of the road bridge in the 1960s; the only minor compensation for the loss is the appearance of pleasant hillocks of birch and heath, interspersed with lawns and densely-planted crocuses and daffodils on land which has probably not supported plant life since before the last ice age.

The name of Victoria is familiar to most Dundonians through Victoria Road, now part of the inner ring road but originally constructed to give access to the north of the city by avoiding the unduly steep Hilltown. Victoria Road was built as a result of the Dundee Improvement Act of 1871; it followed the line of the old Bucklemaker Wynd, which had become something of a slum area but whose name is a reminder of the days before shoelaces displaced buckles, and of the eminence of Dundee in an earlier period in the manufacture of saddlery, sword-belts, straps and scarf-pins. Victoria Road, on a good day, is a sunny and pleasant place; the imposing Scots Baronial factory-buildings on the north side have been renovated and saved for posterity, and the new flats to the south are a good example of piecemeal urban regeneration.

The royal title, if not the name, is commemorated in the Queen's Hotel, a Victorian Gothic pile of the 1870s; built speculatively to meet the needs of the users of the new Caledonian railway, the developers suffered a severe shock when the terminus was finally located half a mile further east, on a site not far from the present Taybridge station. The hotel never quite recovered from this initial blow, but is nevertheless a striking reminder of the new Victorian prosperity. The Queen in 1892 conferred on Dundee the title and status of a city—not before time—with a Lord Provost of its very own. The most recent tribute to the long-lived sovereign is Victoria Park, which dates from 1906.

The earliest piece of royal nomenclature in Dundee is Pitalpin Road, named after the king of the Scots, documentary evidence of whose existence is rather nebulous (see **King's Cross**). Between the sixth century and the nineteenth, however, Dundee seems to have been somewhat lukewarm in its enthusiasm for adopting the names of reigning monarchs; King Street, Queen Street and Princes Street have royal connotations but name no names (see under **Albert**). An exception must however be made of Victoria's predecessor on the throne; though perhaps not universally admired, he was considered in radical Dundee to be such an outstanding leader in the movement for parliamentary reform that a new wet dock, constructed in 1832, was named King William IV Dock. A little street leading to the graving dock is now his only memorial, the dock itself having been filled in to accommodate the landfall of the road bridge in the 1960s.

Wallace

The known facts about the life of William Wallace—Guardian of the Realm, Scottish patriot *par excellence* and *terror Anglorum*—are few but reasonably well-established. Born around 1274, the younger son of a Clydesdale laird, he became the focus of Scottish resistance to the domineering claims of Edward I of England. He won a major victory over an English army at Stirling Bridge in 1297, but after his defeat at Falkirk a year later he had to resort to guerilla tactics, was betrayed to the English, and after a show trial at Westminster was executed with all the savagery of the law in 1305. He left no known descendants.

Dundee has always liked to claim Wallace as one of her own sons, but the facts of the Tayside connection are not so easy to establish. 'Blin' Harry' the Minstrel in his poem *The Wallace* (written in the late fifteenth century) avers that 'In till Dundee Wallace to school they send...'; this is quite likely, since a school was indeed founded here in 1224, and enjoyed more than local fame, but to claim that this was the grammar school which was one of the precursors of Dundee High School involves a degree of speculation unacceptable to most historians. It is generally believed that Wallace was in Dundee during the enemy occupation of the town; there is a further tradition that he was outlawed and had to flee the town after he had killed Selby, the son of the English overlord, in revenge for some insult or other. This is said to have marked the beginning of the Wars of Independence, and it is certainly the case that Edward I had a particular *animus* against Dundee and its citizens and that he sacked the town in 1296. Thereafter Dundee changed hands several times. There is a local belief that it was on Clatto Moor (the site of the present reservoir) that Wallace encamped with his army before besieging the town and damaging the castle (see **Castle Street**); and another that he left via the West Port at the beginning of his campaign against the English. It is known for certain that Wallace, by a charter of 1298, gave the post of Constable of Dundee Castle to a local man named Alexander Carron; the post later became hereditary, and the family designation was to be 'the Skirmisher' or, in the vernacular, 'Scrymgeour' (see **Scrymgeour**).

There are no other known facts to connect William Wallace with Dundee; and indeed there are no streets or buildings named after the hero. Nevertheless the surname has always been current in these parts and held in some reverence. (It comes from an Anglo-Norman word *waelis* meaning foreign, or Welsh, and in Scotland was used with reference to the inhabitants of the ancient kingdom of Strathclyde, who were of the Cumbric or Welsh race.) There was at one time (until it was culverted) a stream which rose behind the Law and flowed east by Clepington to join the Dens burn (see **Dens**); this was known as the Wallace burn, and it also gave its name to Wallace Craigie, one of the large estates lying outside the mediaeval city (see **Craigie**). Wallacetown was a district on the other side of the Dens burn; the name survives as that of a church, and nearby Wallace Street is of similar origin.

Finally, one must mention the renowned firm of bakers, founded by David Wallace in 1869, and still with several retail outlets in Dundee; indeed at one time the words 'Wallace' and 'peh' were almost inseparable in the salivating mouths of Dundonians.

Ward

'The Ward' was described by an eighteenth-century writer as 'a large inclosed Grass park, Shaddowed round with trees and agreeable walks' and separated from the town centre by a fine hedge; the writer is referring, believe it or not, to what is now Ward Road (see also **Overgate**).

'Ward' is an old Scots word with the primary meaning of 'an enclosed piece of land, chiefly for pasture', and occurs frequently in place-names such as Largoward in Fife; later the word came to mean an administrative division defined mainly for electoral purposes. 'The Ward' extended from Barrack Street westward to the present West Port roundabout and before the eighteenth century was completely unbuilt upon; adjacent to the Meadows, it was probably used for grazing. Industrialisation of the area began in the early 1800s with the erection of the Ward Mill, which was acquired in 1840 by two flax traders named Buist. James Buist died in 1844 but his younger brother Alexander Jefferson Buist continued to trade on his own account until 1867, when he was joined by the brothers William and John Don who ran a spinning and weaving factory in Forfar. Thus was born Don Bros, Buist and Co, one of the leading firms in the linen industry in Dundee.

The Buists, of more genteel origin than many of their rivals, were sons of the manse of Tannadice, where their father had been minister from 1786 to his death in 1845. A.J. Buist was well educated, and destined for the law, but for some unknown reason entered the flax trade. He prospered greatly and survived into the present century; his son J.C. Buist outlived all the Don brothers and their three sons, and continued the firm well into the 1920s.

Buist is an interesting name, common enough in Dundee but practically nowhere else. It is from the French *du bois*, and appears also as Boyce. The Dundee-born historian Hector Boece was from the same stable, and probably pronounced his name as Boyce also. The mill-workers on the other

142

hand would pronounce the name of their boss as 'bist'. The name also had wide currency in Dundee as that of a prestigious firm of furniture-makers.

Don Bros Buist & Co demolished the old Ward Mills in the 1870s and built the existing works in Barrack Street (still within the confines of 'The Ward'). The enterprise flourished in its time, but with the depression of the 1930s the brothers Don retrenched at their Forfar base, leaving the Dundee side to dwindle. The firm is no more, and the derelict mills await re-development. It seems unlikely however that they will be replaced by 'trees and agreeable walks'.

Ward Road itself is a development of the 1860s, never very beautiful but important as part of the city's central network. It extends only from Barrack Street to the West Marketgait; at one time it would have led westwards up Guthrie Street and Brook Street (the line of the old Scourin Burn) but the inner ring road has now made this mode of progress virtually impossible. Ward Road was once one of the busiest in the town centre, but with the mutilation of Barrack Street and Lindsay Street has largely lost its sense of direction. Its only distinguished building is the Ward Road museum, a baroque conception of 1911 which, both externally and internally, serves to brighten up this now neglected corner of Dundee.

Wedderburn

Wedderburn is or was the name of an obscure settlement in Berwickshire and refers to a stream frequented by sheep ('wethers'). Despite its being originally a Border surname, it crops up with surprising frequency in Dundee from the sixteenth century to the present day. Given the small repertoire of Christian names in pre-twentieth century Scotland, it is very difficult to sort out the relationships in this notable family, who seem to have held high office in church and municipality for over two hundred years. We do have knowledge however of a particularly gifted branch of the family, namely the three sons of James Wedderburn, a well-doing merchant who had a property in West Kirk Stile near the Old Steeple. James had a hankering after the reformed doctrines then being promoted on the Continent, and was eventually compelled to take refuge there until his death around 1550, but not before he had imparted his free-thinking principles to his sons James, John and Robert.

James Wedderburn *fils* attended St Leonard's College, St Andrews, then a byword for dangerous reforming tendencies, and became a priest in Dundee; he wrote anti-Papist plays which have never been published but which were performed in the 1550s to enthusiastic audiences at the Playfield, a rudimentary open-air theatre beyond the West Port. John was also in holy orders, but his unorthodox views compelled him to flee to Germany, where he became involved in the Lutheran movement; after a brief return to Dundee he was again obliged to leave, and ended his days in France. Robert, the youngest and most gifted of the brothers, also attended St Andrews, but was at St Mary's College; and after a spell in Paris he published in 1548 a work entitled *The Complaynt of Scotland*, a mocking allegory on the state of the contemporary church (successfully revived at Dundee Rep in the 1990s). He collaborated with John in another book called *The Gude and Godlie Ballads*, a poetical work which derided the abuses of the church and which also contains secular poems of great beauty. Robert later compromised his principles to the extent of becoming Vicar of Dundee and died in the city in 1553. The site of the family home is marked by a plaque at the junction of the High Street and the Nethergate.

Other members of this ubiquitous family figure in the pages of Dundee's story. A Wedderburn was in permanent residence in Denmark in the sixteenth century for the purpose of overseeing Dundee's trading connections with that country. Master Alexander Wedderburn, town clerk of Dundee, also lived in the family house in the Nethergate; his claim to fame is that in 1581 he began to compile a Roll of Freemen or Burgesses of Dundee which, as 'the Lockit Book' is one of the city's historical treasures. Sir Alexander Wedderburn acquired the lands of Blackness around 1650; ten years later he was restored by Charles II to the position of town clerk of Dundee, a post which by now had become almost hereditary in the family. It was another Alexander Wedderburn, who as town clerk, approved the proclamation of James III as king of Great Britain at the market cross in Dundee in 1715. Continuing the family tradition, Sir Alexander Wedderburn, Bart., of Blackness raised recruits for the Glenprosen contingent of the Airlie regiment in the '45; after the failure of that enterprise, his son Robert had to resort to the wilds of the Cat Law in north Angus as a temporary hiding place.

The Wedderburns were great rivals of the **Scrymgeours**, but the two families intermarried extensively, producing the line which eventually established a title to the earldom of Dundee. The Wedderburn estate was (and still is) Birkhill, near Balmerino in North Fife: the Dundee suburb of Birkhill took its name from the estate when feus were given off in 1829.

Our city has not been over-zealous in commemorating the Wedderburns. Wedderburn Street and Wedderburn Place off Strathmartine Road are, one suspects, modern coinages and do not refer to the reformers who earned for Dundee the title of the 'Geneva of Scotland'. But if you are interested in Dundee's poetry and can see past the wretched MacGonagall, look at the

144

Gude and Godly Ballads, which contain some love-poetry of which Dundee ought to be proud.

Wellgate

The Wellgate used correctly to be called 'Well-gait' or 'street leading to the well of the Blessed Maria of Dundee'. Lady Well, to give it its shorter name, lay just outside the burgh boundary, and was made available to the citizenry in 1409 by the largesse of Sir James Scrymgeour of Dudhope. Its spring waters were clear and abundant, and formed the principal source of water for the burgh until 1836. As early as the beginning of the fifteenth century the overflow of the Ladywell was taken by aqueduct to the Friar burn on the west; three hundred years later, pipes were laid to conduct the water to various other wells downstream. It was not until the 1830s that there was even a rudimentary domestic water-supply, the water from the wells being collected each morning by water caddies who distributed it from their carts (one penny for ten gallons). The Lady Well, with its stone surround, remained as an ornament until in 1872 it was culverted to make way for Victoria Road; two years later Lintrathen Loch became the city's first reservoir, and not before time, for the reputation of the Lady Well for purity had been destroyed by the increasing numbers of cases of smallpox, typhoid and gastric fevers. (The name Ladywell was recently revived as that of a roundabout on the new inner ring-road and of the avenue connecting Victoria Road to King Street.)

The Wellgate Port was one of the ten principal gates of the town, of which only one (the Cowgate) now survives; the others, in the words of an eighteenth-century commentator, 'standing useless nuisances upon the streets, were taken down to free the streets of such incumbrances and give them more air'—just about as feeble an excuse as any used in respect of twentieth-century civic vandalism. Because of the steepness of the terrain, the use of the Wellgate as a thoroughfare must always have been severely limited, and certainly unfit for vehicular traffic, which is why the gentler Victoria Road was built. Although the Wellgate contained the fashionable Bain Square, a gazetteer of the 1850s avers that 'many of the alleys are inconveniently and orientally narrow'.

Nevertheless the Wellgate was of some importance, being part of the traditional route through the mediaeval town centre and forming the only access to the Hilltown, Strathmartine and the lands beyond. To quote the gazetteer again, 'it stretches from the shore, through Castle-street, Murraygate, Wellgate, and Bonnethill, upwards of three-quarters of a mile...on market days, a scene of bustling and tumultuous business'.

Of course, the Wellgate as a street no longer exists, having been replaced by an enormous shopping centre. With its stores and restaurants, cinema and libraries, the Wellgate Centre has its admirers, and it affords a degree of comfort to its users unimaginable in former days. But to have stood at the top of the old Wellgate Steps, when the football crowds coming down from Dens or 'Tanners' met the shoppers coming up from the Murraygate was to get a sense of purposeful activity which is not often found in the area nowadays.

Whale Lane

West Whale Lane has been gobbled up by the new Marketgait and East Whale Lane is little more than a car park; even before these developments they were insignificant mini-thoroughfares connecting Dock Street with the Seagate—but their names would have spoken volumes to our grandparents, recalling as they do the great days of one of Dundee's most exciting and picturesque industries. The city may have come in a poor second to Aberdeen during the North Sea oil boom, but in the days of sailing ships Dundee had no rival.

In the period before the development of mineral oils, households depended on fish and animal oils for illumination. The Tay Whale Fishing Company had been formed in the mid-eighteenth century, encouraged by government subsidies; and in 1817 the streets of Dundee were still being lit by oil lamps (twenty-four of them to be exact). Seals and whales being the most prolific source of oil, many of the east coast ports in Britain had small fleets which hunted these mammals in the Arctic seas. But technology was catching up; and a company, later the Dundee Gas Light Company, was formed and bought land to the south of Ferry Road at 'the Crofts', so that by 1826 Dundee with its 35,000 inhabitants was being lit by gas. This was a facility which the city of Paris was not to enjoy for another fourteen years.

There were however other uses for lubricants; and when whale oil was found to be useful in preparing jute, the demand for it grew in Dundee. Until the 1830s Peterhead had been the principal port, but thereafter Dundee crews were pre-eminent in the development of commercial whaling; and it was Whale Lane which was the centre of the oil-related activity. Many of the oil-boiling yards were situated there during the days of whaling, and a nineteenth-century writer recorded that 'the very air was greasy, and the kerbstones were black and oily'. The Dundee whaling fleet kept on expanding, and by the second half of the nineteenth century had become the largest and best-equipped in the country.

In Dundee's boom days the whaling and the jute industries were largely

146

interdependent. Jute fibre was crushed and then treated with an emulsion of oil and water in order to soften it for further processing. Whale oil was at first used in this connection, and the future of both industries seemed secure. There were important spin-offs too: it was the Dundee firm of William Stephen which built the whaling-ship *Narwhal* in 1859. No-one would have guessed that when the same firm, twenty years later, built the *Terra Nova* it was to be the last of the whalers. The reason for the decline in Arctic whaling was simply the scarcity of whales; and an expedition in 1892-3 by the Dundee ship the *Balaena* to the distant seas of the Antarctic failed to give any promise of revival. By the time of the 1914-18 war the industry was fast disappearing.

Dundee no longer has the aura of a seaport; and there is a certain amount of revulsion at the destruction for profit of rare and beautiful creatures such as whales. If we wish to remind ourselves of the boom days of the whaling ships and their daring and intrepid crews we have to rely on such names as Whale Lane and Baffin Street (constructed in 1830 at the height of the whalers' prosperity, and connecting Arbroath Road and Broughty Ferry Road).

Whitehall

There is a persistent tradition, going back at least three hundred years, that Whitehall Close (as it then was) was the site of the 'Antient Palace' of Dundee. When King Malcolm III married the English princess Margaret in 1070, so the story goes, a palace was built for them in what is now the High Street; a nearby close was said to have been named St Margaret's in consequence (but there is no evidence for any of this). A century later William the Lion, wishing to consolidate his power in Scotland, made large grants of land to his brother David earl of Huntingdon, including the burgh of Dundee. Earl David thereafter referred to Dundee as 'my burgh', and one of his first acts was the construction of a great church dedicated to the Virgin Mary (see **St Mary's**); in addition he was able to obtain, through networking in the south, considerable trading privileges for 'his' burgh. (Despite this, there has never been a Dundee place-name that refers either to David or to Huntingdon.)

The whereabouts of the earl's habitation are unknown, but he is stated to have occupied a property in the Flukergate (see **Nethergate**) close to the shore-path, and as late as 1496 the remains of a structure were referred to as 'Erle David Huntletoun's Haw' [hall]. It must be assumed that his brother King William resided in Dundee from time to time, either in this building or in the castle of Dundee (see under **Castle**). The language of the Scottish

147

court at this time and for the next two centuries was Norman French, and it is not surprising that there should be a reference in a mediaeval French romance to a royal *palais* in the burgh; but this is necessarily ambiguous, and could equally refer to David's 'Haw' or to the great hall of the castle.

The first (anonymous) history of Dundee written in 1776 states baldly '…the King's Palace stood a little to the North and west of the High Street …After the Kings gave over coming to reside in this Town, it became the dwelling place of the Earls of Angus, And afterwards of the Viscounts Dudhop'. This merely adds to the confusion, for it is known that the viscounts built their residence a mile from the town centre (see **Dudhope**). The *Gazetteer of Scotland* of 1848 repeats the story of a royal residence in Dundee, and adds that there was also in the vicinity a mint in which coin was struck in the 1390s during the reign of Robert III.

Later historians have tended to discredit the notion of an official royal residence in Dundee; there is no evidence that King Edgar ever stayed in Dundee, far less that he died there in 1107. And as 'Whitehall' did not really enter the Scottish consciousness until after the union of the crowns in 1603, the name seems irrelevant to a consideration of the 'Antient Palace' theory.

The truth about the origin of Dundee's Whitehall seems to be as follows: the area now occupied by Whitehall Street (a late nineteenth-century thoroughfare) was intersected by two very old closes, one of which dated from the foundation of the burgh. On the west of it stood the above-mentioned hall belonging to the earl David, probably built around 1200 and removed at some time during the later mediaeval period. The other close belonged in the sixteenth century to a wealthy burgess named George Spens who built several town houses on the site, one of which fell into the possession of a member of the staunchly royalist Strathmore family, Sir Patrick Lyon by name; Sir Patrick at the restoration of Charles II in 1660 changed the name of his house to 'Whitehall' (the London home of his royal master), and arranged for a set of sculptured arms to be placed above the doorway, with the motto 'God Save The King, C.R. 1660'. When the close was swept away in 1883 the arms were removed to a museum formerly housed in the Old Steeple.

In the nineteenth century, the area of Whitehall Close had become one of Dundee's blackspots, a huddle of dirty and smelly houses 'where fever and death walked arm in arm, and contributed largely to the silent population of the Howff' as an early guide-book picturesquely puts it. The old close was replaced by a street of some elegance, with notable shops adorned by distinguished family-names such as Draffen, Kidd and Justice, and still one of the city's best shopping areas; Whitehall Crescent, with the Gilfillan Church as its centrepiece,was an ambitious conception on the lines of London's Aldwych, now stultified by the new road system and overlooked by the intrusive Tayside House, the local authority headquarters.

Wishart

George Wishart (1514-1546) was not a native Dundonian and did not live in the town for any length of time; yet he was perhaps the greatest Reformer of his age and before his death one of the best-loved pastors of Dundee. His most conspicuous memorial is the East or Cowgate Port, always known as the Wishart Arch from the circumstance of his having preached there.

The Cowgate, once, along with the Seagate, the principal street in the mediaeval town, has alas been marginalised and is now a dead end (see under **Murraygate**). The old gateway still exists, but it is now off the beaten track, standing in isolation like a miniature and melancholy Arc de Triomphe, overlooked by decaying warehouses. It is clear from its construction that it was intended more as a checkpoint than a defence, but it is still a notable historical monument and worthy of a better setting; it would almost certainly have been demolished had it not been for its legendary association with the preacher. (The whole area is in fact desolate and run down: the Wishart Memorial Church in King Street has lost its congregation, and its sightless windows are covered in pigeon-droppings—this is the church in whose Sunday School Mary Slessor taught—but who nowadays remembers the common factory girl who was later to go as a missionary to one of the most savage and pestilential parts of Africa?)

Wishart was born near Montrose and educated there, and became a schoolmaster in the town after attending King's College, Aberdeen. Inspired by the new reformed doctrines, he turned preacher and spent some time on the Continent before returning to his native country to spread the by now heretical word. From contemporary accounts he seems to have looked like the Hollywood idea of a Scotch preacher—tall of stature, melancholy of visage, with a long black gown which matched his flowing beard, and a broad Scots accent. But what he preached was not hellfire but comfort and reconciliation, and on his return to Dundee (in defiance of a government veto) he became a hero to the plague-stricken populace to whom he ministered with selfless devotion. The persistent theory that it was from the 'Wishart Arch' that he preached has never been completely verified, for the actual location and date of the existing East port are a matter of some doubt. Nevertheless, a brass plaque on the structure confidently repeats the assertion of John Knox (his contemporary) that 'during the plague of 1544 George Wishart preached from the parapet of this Port. The people standing within the Gate and the Plague-stricken lying without in booths'.

The religious establishment had become nervous about the activities of free-thinking clerics, and Wishart had overstepped the mark with his anti-papist teachings. The clergy led by the powerful Cardinal Beaton resolved to have him removed. The story goes that an attempt was made on his life near the Cowgate Port, but that Wishart somehow survived it (and even helped his would-be assassin to escape from the enraged mob). But in 1546 Wishart was betrayed into the hands of the Cardinal, and after a show trial in the cathedral of St Andrews was burned at the stake outside the nearby castle (where the initials GW on the pavement helpfully identify the spot).

There had also been in circulation a trumped-up charge that Wishart was plotting the death of Cardinal Beaton; but this is almost certainly a case of mistaken identity. For one thing, Wishart came of a large and influential Angus family, at least one of whose members shared his forename; for another, a talent for conspiracy seems most unlikely in this unworldly man. Wishart is said also to have foretold the death of Beaton, a prophecy which was duly fulfilled two months later when a band of assassins gained entry to the very same castle and barbarously knifed the Cardinal to death; Wishart's supporters were involved, but it was much more than a revenge killing.

The story does not have a happy ending, for only a few years later in 1547 the English army of Henry VIII, after their victory at Pinkie, sacked Dundee. The reform movement had become caught up in international politics, and at a grievous cost in human suffering.

150

Envoi

You will perhaps have noticed the scrupulous avoidance of the first person singular in this little book—achieved sometimes at the expense of stylistic ease. Perhaps I may now break this self-imposed rule and describe what made me put pen to paper.

I am of course a Dundonian born and bred, with an intense love of the city of my boyhood and its people. I was born and brought up in the house which has now become the Angus Nursing Home. On either side were large Victorian mansions with huge gardens and a tennis court apiece. Even in my early childhood these houses had become somewhat decrepit, and were about to be divided into flats. Less than 500 yards away were the jute mills in Thomson Street, which I traversed several times daily on my way to and from school or when being sent for 'messages' to the Perth Road. I remember the factory girls with their dust-covered clothes and the strong men leading or backing the horses and carts laden with jute, and I heard their (usually cheerful and always colourful) conversations. Thus it was that I acquired early on an ear and a fascination for the local dialect—not a very useful accomplishment, since I would never have dared to converse in Dundonese with a genuine native speaker. In adult life I have wished many a time that I could have gone into the factories to see what was going on and to make the acquaintance of the workers: but 12-year-old boys in those days were shy, and my presence would not in any event have been welcomed. And how could I have been expected to know that in a few years all would be changed and even the dialect obsolescent?

I left Dundee at the age of 25 to undertake National Service, and have since neither lived nor worked in the city. And now as a pensioner resident in another county I am subject to the nostalgia induced both by age and by long (if not continual) absence.

Nostalgia can be irritating to the young and to those who have never been away, and if this is combined with criticism of the present-day state of things it can be well-nigh intolerable. If in places I have been over-critical I apologise. But it does seem to me that although Dundee has coped as well as most industrial cities with the sweeping changes of the past fifty years, an awful lot has been unnecessarily lost.

It is of course natural that I should be dismayed not only by change but by the fact that nowadays in Dundee I all too rarely meet anyone that I know. A stroll down Reform Street and up the Nethergate to the University used to yield a dozen chance encounters, but now my attention is free to notice once again the disappearance of the Kinnaird Cinema and Green's Playhouse, not to speak of the sorry mess that lies between what was the foot of Lindsay Street and Long Wynd. I don't expect to see tramcars with the old familiar names like 'Hyndford Street' or 'Balgay Road', but I confess to surprise at seeing buses with destinations such as 'Mill o' Mains' or even 'Tesco'.

Dundee's long history has had its ups and downs and the poor old town has been besieged, burnt, devastated and defaced more than most places have a right to expect. Lord Cockburn noted that Dundee in the mid-nineteenth century was 'a sink of atrocity, which no moral flushing seems capable of cleansing'—but he was wrong, was he not? The jute booms which followed were interspersed by severe depressions (the unemployment rate in the industry in 1931 was 50%) and shipbuilding and jam-making seem to have gone for ever. Terrible mistakes have been made: not only the demolition of the charming town hall (in 1931, the year of my birth) but the fact of its having been sited in such a congested area in the first place (and, would you believe it, with a north-facing piazza?). And the Overgate development, although possibly acceptable in the 1960s when vertical concrete blocks were the latest art-form, really must give place to something more worthy to be a backdrop to Dundee's gracious city churches and magnificent Old Steeple.

If you remember as I do the broad pavements of the old Nethergate, with their Victorian townhouses converted into shops (like Phins the ironmongers) and the curve of Lindsay Street as it swept past the lawns and gardens of the city churches towards the High Street, you may ask yourself—how did we allow all this to be swept away? The answer of course is that ring roads and one-way systems were necessitated by the vast increase in the volume of traffic, and without them the city's arteries would by now have succumbed to a massive thrombosis. The road bridge is a symptom and not the main cause of the problem; and being a commuter bridge its landfall could hardly have avoided being near the centre. When, despite all the ingenuity of the planners, fatal infarction occurs in the traffic system, we may yet see a return to a pedestrianised centre worthy of the chief city of Angus.

Ideas on civic development have changed radically in the past half-century: it used to be the philosophy in Dundee (as elsewhere) that the systematic removal of nearly all building over a century old should be the basis of long-term civic planning; and had not the 1939 war intervened this might well have happened here on a large scale. Now we are prepared to remove what is obsolete or just plain bad—and there still remain numerous parts of Dundee which are in that category. Attempts have also been made, through the provision of sheltered housing on some of the former mill sites near the centre, to halt the inexorable move to the periphery which was making a ghost town of Dundee. Other mill sites have been developed in imaginative ways, in particular Verdant Works, turned by Dundee's Heritage Trust into a fascinating museum which effortlessly introduces the visitor to the World of Jute.

The creation in 1982 of Dundee's Enterprise Zone was responsible for two new industrial estates, a High Technology Park, an airport and a waterfront development; it is possible to feel confident that this impetus will continue. To end on a somewhat optimistic note, I rejoice in the modernisation of some of the dreary parts of our old city and welcome the exciting new developments that we are witnessing in the fields of education, technology, the arts, health care and financial enterprise.

I am grateful to all the friends, relatives and acquaintances—too numerous to mention—who have contributed their comments and ideas to this book. I have not come across a single person who has been unwilling to talk affectionately and at length about Dundee—which is really all that I have been doing for the last 150 pages.